Tears of Christepona

Tears of Christepona

Mystical Musings on Grief, Evil, and Godding

Carter Heyward

RESOURCE *Publications* • Eugene, Oregon

TEARS OF CHRISTEPONA
Mystical Musings on Grief, Evil, and Godding

Copyright © 2021 Carter Heyward. All rights reserved. Except for brief quotations in critical publications or reviews, no part of this book may be reproduced in any manner without prior written permission from the publisher. Write: Permissions, Wipf and Stock Publishers, 199 W. 8th Ave., Suite 3, Eugene, OR 97401.

Resource Publications
An Imprint of Wipf and Stock Publishers
199 W. 8th Ave., Suite 3
Eugene, OR 97401

www.wipfandstock.com

PAPERBACK ISBN: 978-1-6667-1366-4
HARDCOVER ISBN: 978-1-6667-1367-1
EBOOK ISBN: 978-1-6667-1368-8

10/08/21

this one's for you, Bev

What is imagination if not a window into God?
—Sr. Angela, CC[1]

---

1. In conversation with the author, Community of Clare, Stroud, NSW, Australia, January, 1991.

Contents

Preface | ix
Prologue | xiii
Acknowledgments | xvii

Theological Intuition | 1
Christepona | 4
Christepona Introduces Herself/Themselves | 7
Arrival of COVID-19 | 12
Feather and Carter | 14
Tenderness and Anger | 18
Time Is Up | 21
Time and Eternity | 25
Buying Time? | 28
Mutuality: The Core of Goodness/God/Godding | 32
Evil | 35
Christofascism | 37
Justice-love: Beyond Sentiment | 42
Empathy, Kindness, Compassion, Courage | 45
Hate: A Wasted Emotion | 48
Faith: Driving the Future | 53
Intuition and Reason | 55
Capitalist Spirituality | 58
Turning to Jesus | 63
A Universal Spirit of Mutual Respect—Simply Utopic? | 69

Tears | 75
Aftermath | 78
Forgiveness | 79
Prayer of Christepona | 83
Joy and Sorrow | 87
Old Dog Bailey | 89
Hunger, Thirst, and Addiction | 91
Suffering and Apathy | 96
Immigrants, Refugees, Borders, and "the Other" | 99
What Churches Should Be Preaching, Teaching, and Doing about Immigration | 104
Winter Trees: Metaphorical Musing | 108
White Supremacy Hangs On | 110
Time Out: Prayer | 114
Time In: Meditation | 116
The Tragedy of Misogyny | 118
Nonbinary Gender and Sexuality | 125
Savagery | 129
Truth and Lies | 131
Aging and Old-Soul | 135
In Memoriam | 140

Bibliography | 141

Preface

It all began when I reached back into my past and reread *The Prophet* (1923) by Lebanese-American Kahlil Gibran (1883 to 1931). The small book, much beloved around the world, reported an imaginary conversation between the prophet Al Mustapha and the people on a fictional island. It became almost immediately a popular hit and, over the next half century, emerged as one of the bestselling books in the world. Still, *The Prophet* was never taken seriously by most literary critics in the West, who considered it too "low-brow," the light-weight fluff of an amorphous spirituality, a dismissal all too familiar to many women theologians, spiritual teachers, and other writers and artists.

The Prophet reflects no one tradition but rather several, much in keeping with the Baha'i faith that had made an enormous impact on the Christian Gibran, as had the Sufi tradition within Islam. The only connection I dare draw between Gibran's work in *The Prophet* and mine in *Tears of Christepona* is our common passion to give voice to an active spiritual power that transcends any one tradition and moves us beyond ourselves into something greater.

I finished writing this book in January 2020, almost a year before the decisive defeat of an authoritarian US president in tandem with the violent rise of his white supremacist followers. Their assault on the US Capitol and Congress sitting in session, on January 6, 2021, was inevitable, given the president's panicked and persistent lie about the so-called "fraudulent" election which he had lost, a lie compounding his lies about himself and just about everything else throughout his presidency and perhaps his life. But enough about Donald J. Trump, whose name appears only occasionally in this book, because it is not all about him.

I wrote most of these reflections back when I was supporting Elizabeth Warren for president, which now seems light years before the inauguration of Joe Biden and Kamala Harris on January 20, 2021, a date I celebrated along with much of the justice-loving world.

I had completed the original manuscript shortly before the coronavirus pandemic was publicly recognized in the United States and months before its economic partner of devastation and suffering had become a global backdrop to our common life, though I made some revisions to the book as the pandemic set in among us in early spring 2020.

I had finished this project about four months before the murder of George Floyd on May 25, 2020, and the consequent revitalization of Black Lives Matter as an irrepressible national movement, in which I became an organizer of our local NAACP's weekly "Moral Monday" BLM witness in the center of our small mountain town.

I tell you this because, in terms of *chronos*—the time via calendars and clocks—the book in your hands is somewhat untimely. And yet, as I will suggest in what follows, in *kairos*—the timelessness in which all that is most important in our lives is uplifted and shaped—the good and the bad, the sad and the glad, this book may have arrived just in time.

Upon rereading the manuscript a year after its completion, I decided to insert occasional notes on how more recent events have illustrated, challenged, reinforced, or shown my earlier reflections to be short-sighted or mistaken. In each case, the additional material is inserted in the body of the text simply as a "2021 note."

Tears of Christepona is a manifesto of consciousness and faith that stretches beyond the rational and empirical. Spiritual seekers and others open to mystery, mysticism, or magic may find it refreshing. I hope to energize you and encourage you to listen well and tell your own stories of how and when you too may have wrestled with angels, because that is what is happening here.

PREFACE

Like any book, this one is not for everyone. Those whose beliefs are structured largely around reason and verifiability may want to stop here. Those for whom "theology" is largely an academic study of mostly white and mostly male thinkers may have little interest in what I am doing here. Those for whom politics and spirituality are separate realms of effort and inquiry will not likely want to waste their time on these musings in which the realms coalesce.

Indeed, there are several ways skeptics can, if they wish, set this book aside. They can dismiss it as the outpourings of a grief-stricken older woman, which it is. They can shelve it as the spiritual assault of a feminist priest on the patriarchal logic of Christianity, which it is. They can roll their eyes at the author's hostility toward the advanced capitalist and white supremacist toxins that infuse the air she breathes and which, she apparently believes, have sickened her soul—and theirs too, regardless of their race, but especially if they're white. They can assume that these massive evil structures against which she beats her head have rattled her brain, leaving her a little goofy, or just plain nuts. But this, I can promise you, is not the case.

These pages emerged in anger and hope—more interestingly, the book bears witness to voices of outrageous love. And while there are perfectly good reasons for people to shut this book now and move on, try to remember that what we choose not to observe is sometimes what we most need to see, and that right behind the door we close is where the key to what we are seeking may be hidden. Who knows?

Do I imagine that this is the best, much less only, place that seekers may discover some spiritual truth or political guideposts that might be useful? Of course not. Never, ever, is there only one of us speaking the truth, however partially. This is one small book, written by one woman, brimming over with sorrow and joy, disappointment and hope, anger and gratitude, and who is speaking to those who may turn these pages in a spirit of openness, curiosity, hope, and perhaps also, with me, occasionally in tears.

Prologue

I GAVE MY LIFE to Christ when I was fourteen at a Billy Graham rally in the Charlotte, North Carolina, Coliseum. Fifteen years later, on July 29, 1974, along with ten other women, I was ordained prior to the Episcopal Church's authorization of women priests. From that day on, the "Philadelphia Eleven" were deemed "irregular" women priests, a branding we grew into. Celebrating birthday number seventy-five in 2020, I'm imagining that the spontaneous spiritual step I took with Mr. Graham back in 1959, followed by a more well-considered leap with my sister priests in 1974, together with a joyful discovery in the 2000s that horses are among my most reliable priests, have led me along a path of spiritual liberation through social and political upheaval.

But how to communicate this, how to extend such conversation beyond myself and my closest friends and colleagues, including my animal companions? A little background to this quandary:

My first book (1976), on the ordination of women priests, was shelved in a Berkeley, California, bookstore under the rubric of "the occult." My second book (1982), on the radically mutual relationality at the core of God, could not find a publisher for about a year because, I was told, it was too Christian for non-Christians and not Christian enough for Christians; too feminist for nonfeminists and not feminist enough for feminists; too academic for a popular readership and not academic enough for religious scholars. And only recently, in 2020, I was told by a distinguished editor that, although this book in your hands has a readership, including his own daughter, his liberal Christian press cannot take it because it's not a good fit with its list, point being it won't sell.

PROLOGUE

My awkward journey as a marketable writer-theologian suggests that not only my writings, but my life as a whole, falls outside the boxes, categories, and "identities" by which things and people are advertised and sold. Along with many of you, I fall between the cracks of such categories of identity as gender, religion, class, and culture; and such categories of professional interest and personal competence as religious studies, psychology, politics, social and economic theory.

While it may be to our credit that we aren't easily typecast, it makes reaching each other more challenging in a world in which not to easily fit is not to easily be found. Yet here we are, having found each other.

Tears of Christepona is an attempt to reach folks who also fall somewhere between this and that. And if what I am communicating already rings a bell of truth for you or sparks some interest, what is spoken here may encourage you to speak more freely—or at least bolster your self-confidence—in the midst of the disruptive convergence of political upheaval, moral crisis, and the tumultuous arrival of COVID-19, which broke into our lives a couple of months after I had mostly completed the first draft of this book in January 2020.

The coronavirus crisis has required me to reread and rewrite, deepening and stretching my point of view—much as the crisis has affected how many of us see ourselves, the world around us, and the spaces between us in this strange, challenging time. COVID-19 may be pushing many of us personally beyond the brink of how we've heretofore made sense of ourselves and one another. With whom can we be in touch, and what does being "in touch" even mean in social spaces in which we cannot touch each other? Who's at high risk to get sick and even die? Why is the reliance on science so controversial at this time? Who's economically secure enough in this crisis? And what is "enough" in the world of COVID? What differences do our genders, sexualities, racial identities, languages, and ages, make in relation to the coronavirus? This virus may be tossing us all between the cracks of this and that—and especially perhaps between our experiences of time as we ordinarily experience its

PROLOGUE

linear movement from one minute or day to the next and time as a more liminal experience of movement in circles, spirals, or even as our being somehow suspended in time, moving in patterns heretofore unknown to us, not all that clear what day it is and how it may differ from yesterday or tomorrow.

Acknowledgments

DEEP APPRECIATION TO BK Hipsher and Devon Lerner, who helped me edit and shape this book and brainstormed with me about publishing and marketing possibilities. I am grateful, of course, for the confidence of Matt Wimer, Chelsea Lobey, Calvin Jaffarian, Mike Surber, and other editors at Wipf and Stock/Resource Publications in Eugene, Oregon, who accepted the manuscript and have worked with me to bring it to you. Thanks also to several colleagues who read the manuscript in earlier drafts before I thought I would find a publisher for something so different from anything I've ever imagined writing: Pedro A. Sandin-Fremaint, Anne Bathurst Gilson, Alla Renee Bozarth, Darlene O'Dell, Robin Hawley Gorsline, and Peace Lee.

Some folks dear to me encouraged this book in ways they may not realize, or then again they may: Rob Drinkwater, Isabel Drinkwater, and Kate Alexander Heyward, nephew and nieces whose courage and common sense give me hope; Darlene O'Dell, who lives, teaches, and writes the truth, regardless; Liz Galloway, cherished feisty friend forever; Gerry Azzata, sister animal-lover, music-lover, and political soulmate; Josh Rood, whose friendship and farm-help has been beyond value; Sandi Thompson, whose knowledge of horses and enduring friendship is priceless; Danielle Howard and Suzanne Fairbairn, dog-lovers, great helpers, and fine friends; Marsha Carter Davis, wonderfully creative cousin; Amy Perry Carter, whose photographs reflect such kindness; Albert Dulin, a most beloved friend, with whom relational roots go deep; Kris Woodaman, remarkable equine vet, with whom roots also go deep; Hilary Dirlam, good friend and great teacher of fiddle and ancient wisdom; Judith Davis, Anne Gilson, Ann Franklin, and Elly Andujar, friends for the ages; Barbara Gerlach, Emily Jean Gilbert, Susan Savell, Sarah Bentley, Maurine Doggett, and Linda Clark, sister-sojourners through sorrows and joys for over half a century; Kathleen Barnes, Sheila Mooney, and Susan Lefler, NAACP colleagues who've helped me and each other stay awake and more or less sane in these challenging times; Jody Ralston, with whom I walk and talk almost daily, sister-friend at the farm, and chief caregiver for the horses; Norene Carter, brave friend of many years who shares a passion for justice and animals; Gretchen Grimshaw, sister priest, lover of dogs and horses, and theologian like none other; Sheila Baker, who cuts my hair, cuddles my dog, and talks sane, passionate politics with me every six weeks; Jenn Rouse, Gerrie Kiley, and Nancy Richards, bold and bright sister adventurers at Redbud Springs, each a source of a special and unique wisdom; Eva Cavros, Kim Keifrider, and Alan Paduano, my holy trinity of body-healers; Betsy Alexander and Robert Dulin, whose inspiration in my life grows ever stronger; and Marsha Knott Carter, whose radiant beauty is for me an image of "Christepona."

Finally, love and gratitude way beyond words to Ann Heyward, Robbie Heyward, Jan Surrey, Jim Lewis, David Conolly, and Angela Moloney, my closest spiritual companions still walking on this earth—and to Sue Sasser, ever-abundant source of love, humor, and wisdom.

Theological Intuition

WHEN I'M ASKED WHICH of my books a reader might want to start with, I often point to *The Redemption of God: A Theology of Mutual Relation* (1982), my doctoral thesis because it provides the basis for everything I've ever written or spoken about God. In it I examine my intuitive childhood hunches that God is not an overseer of some sort, not a father or mother, not a king or queen, not a lord or ruler or big man in control of history; and that God is not an entirely "other" being from us at all, not an "entity" who lives apart from us, above or outside us humans and other creatures.

By the time I was about five years old, something had "told" me that this spirit that folks at home and in church called "God" was not only very real and very powerful but also was everywhere and all around and always present, trying somehow to reach us and speak to us and help us do the right thing. The God of my childhood was as alive as you and me, a ubiquitous spirit of kindness and justice-love and forgiveness and joy. In aging, I find myself wishing I could thank Bob and Mary Ann for the breadth and depth of their spiritual intuitions and parental wisdom, for I have no doubt that my most reliable spirituality and religious thinking springs from my childhood home and the parental permission to think my own thoughts and try to be kind to everyone, human and other creatures as well. As you will see, my desire to somehow connect with Mary Ann and Bob apparently has helped shape the content of these pages.

Throughout much of my life, as a child and young woman and later as a professional theologian, I've wrestled in my head and heart with how on earth to understand a profoundly good, justice-loving spirit of kindness, compassion, and courage in relation to the cruelty, greed, and violence that seem so overwhelming in the world and throughout history. What do we make of the relation between God and evil?

My friend and theological mentor Dorothee Soelle once put it something like this in conversation: if God is good, God is not powerful. If God is powerful, God is not good. Of course, Dorothee was using "powerful" as synonymous with "omnipotent," almighty, having all authority, being in control, exercising absolute power over the world.

With Dorothee and many other spiritual leaders and theological teachers and students in the late twentieth century, I would come to believe that God's power is not "power-over" but rather is "power-with," and that power-with is what Jesus and many other spiritual teachers have called "love."

Love is always, and everywhere, most clearly experienced and expressed as sharing power, not hoarding or withholding, and certainly not wielding power over others. This would lead me to assert in *The Redemption of God* that "mutuality"—shared power, power-with one another—is sacred power, God's power, and that, indeed, God comes to life forever and ever through the mutuality we generate with one another: with humans, with other creatures, and with God's own spirit.

I would come to believe that the struggle of God against evil is rooted historically in tension between those who experience love as sharing, power-with others, and those for whom power is by definition the wielding of power-over others. This stubborn belief has helped ground my life and work over decades as a white lesbian Christian feminist theologian of liberation.

Not by any means do I assume that I personally am always on the good side, the God side, the "power-with" side, the justice-love-making side, of history or my own story. Clearly, and shamefully, this has not always been the case for me personally or for my ancestors and family. The greed and violence embedded in white supremacy, misogyny, class elitism, hatred of "others," disregard of the earth and its creatures, xenophobias of many kinds, and historic structures of evil, live on through even the best intentioned of us in these times and this world. Certainly, various personal insecurities, failures, and choices not to love haunt my life as they do all spiritually honest humans.

But thanks to good parenting and teaching, as well as good modeling from friends and mentors, and certainly from the sacred God-spirit we meet in our soul as conscience, I can tell what is good, or God, and what is evil in many situations, and I also notice that good and evil are mixed and scrambled together in most real-life contexts, because human motive is always a factor, and our motives are usually mixed. And so I write with some confidence, and much humility, about the struggles between good and evil in which we find ourselves today.

None of what I have written above will be either new or surprising to anyone familiar with my work. What is new, and what may surprise everyone, even those who know me best, is the voice of Christepona who authors this book with and through me.

Christepona

CHRISTEPONA IS THE VOICE of God of many names, images, species, cultures, and religions, including Christianity at its most inclusive, justice-loving best.

Christepona is also a gift of intuition and imagination and reason. Psychologists might call her my superego or our collective unconscious. Moralists might hear her as my conscience, or ours. Spiritualists might assume that she is an angel, perhaps even a host of angels.

Christepona, I am certain, is also the voice of ancestors, family, and friends of different species whom I have known and loved, and surely also of many human and other creatures I haven't known or loved. That is to say, Christepona is the voice of the communion of saints, those gone before us who have spiritual wisdom to share with us and through us as we carry them on in history.

But Christepona is not only the voice of God and the voice of the saints. Christepona's voice is also my voice, Carter Heyward's voice, when I am speaking most truthfully. Christepona is me at my best, the way I was, and am, created to be most fully human. You might say that in talking with Christepona, I am talking to myself, my best self, which just might be a way of imaging what it means to be in touch with the Spirit, God, who speaks to us and who we can sometimes hear if we are listening.

Christepona's voice also might suggest something about who you, the reader/listener, are created to be when you are most fully yourselves, at your best. Indeed, I believe that Christepona speaks for us all at our best—that is, how we are created to be through, and by, a Spirit-God of mutuality that infuses us all with the power to love.

Do not be confused. I am not suggesting that you and I will hear the exact same voice, or voices, when we are most in touch with our better angels, our best selves, the Sacred Spirit or spirits as she, he, or they speak to us. Our diversities evoke different voices, cultural codes, and abilities among us to hear. We are not the same and God forbid that we try to be. But I am suggesting as emphatically as I can that the content of the message, the substance of God's words and voices, does not vary that much among the humans on this planet when it comes to making justice-love and building peace and exercising empathy and tenderness where we can and anger at oppression and violence wherever we find it or it finds us. Neighbor-love is a universal spiritual call and moral mandate. The shapes and languages vary, the substance, the call to love, is constant. That message is at the heart of this book.

As a Christian, I do indeed imagine that Christepona's is the voice of Jesus of Nazareth, a "christic" voice meant to be shared, eternally evoking our capacities to generate neighbor-love, or power-with one another, to heal broken lives and transform the world.

With "Christ" as a basis of her name, Christepona is not interested in becoming the centerpiece of anyone's spirituality or consciousness. She is the transcendent spirit of connection, a relational energy of mutuality that crosses over among and between all of us and our belief systems.

Christepona is both deeply personal and radically transpersonal and political. She is psychologically healing, socially transformative, and politically a source of revolutionary patience.[1]

Christepona knows no boundaries, no boxes, no categories, no religions, and no limits to who or what she or he or they or it or we can be among us, for us, with us, between and among us.

Christepona is whoever and whatever calls you and me to live most fully and truthfully, with kindness toward all, and

---

1. Soelle, *Revolutionary Patience*.

courage to reach out beyond ourselves in healing and transforming the world around us.

My introduction of Christepona in these pages may signal to you, the reader, that I am either crazy, exactly like many women, witches, heretics have been in history, or that I am in touch here with our sacred source, or both. I can assure you that writing this book has radicalized my own understandings of madness, myself, and God. One of the lessons I have learned is that, through the eyes of God—Christepona—I am an utterly common woman, unique as each of us is, but not exceptional at my core. I am with you and, truth to tell, with all creatures, with more in common than we normally realize.

"So let's get on with it, dahling," Sister Angela from the Community of Clare in Stroud, New South Wales, Australia, would often say when she was ready to move on. Now.

Christepona Introduces Herself/Themselves

NOVEMBER 9, 2019. I awoke to a sorrowful sound, wailing for a split second, but then I heard a shout of urgency. Strangely, the voice seemed to come from deep inside me and yet from beyond me too.

Who are you? I asked silently.

Was I talking to myself or someone else?

Only silence in response. I stretched my legs out and put my hands over my eyes. Had I only imagined I heard it, a voice?

Who are you? I asked again, this time sort of out loud, I think. Who are you? What's going on?

At least a minute passed, and probably another. Then she or he or it or they, or something, spoke, slowly, clearly.

We are whoever you need us to be, Carter—whoever you need us to be to bolster your confidence, root your empathy, ground your compassion, secure your courage. Our names are as many as could ever be imagined by all beings in all waking or dreaming moments of your lives. Call us whatever is truest to your spiritual need at this time. You know who we are. Our name reflects your deepest knowledge of who we are. You can't deny us and be true to yourself or us.

I thought in silence for what seemed to be a long time, a minute or so at least—What's going on? What or who am I hearing? Why do these words seem to be my own, yet coming from somewhere beyond me?

I wondered, still in silence: Am I hearing Sophia-Wisdom whom I came to know best through my beloved friend and sister priest Alison, whose memorial we just last week celebrated?

Or am I hearing Angela, my soulmate from years back who still laughs with me and rides the horses with us and reminds me almost daily of the silliness of religious pomposity and of the powerfully transformative character of the most truthful and loving spiritualities regardless of religion. Sister Angela, after all, once said that imagination is a "window into God."

I sighed and lay still, thinking, stretching my mind and body and heart. I need Sophia's wisdom and I certainly need Angela to wrap her massive angel-arms around me, or Alison to laugh with me right now, or Bev to listen and speak.

Moments, maybe minutes, passed.

Silence.

Then I heard myself exclaim, "My God!"

And through the silence it rang—the voice, clear as the sharpest bell.

Of course, we are each of these dear ones and many more. But right now an honest and helpful image of who we are for you might be "Christepona," she who is present in all living beings. We meet you today most urgently in the spirit of our Jewish sibling from Nazareth and we also come to you through your mare Red and her daughter Feather, whom you have just learned is sick and who needs your special care and healing touch.

Let us, Christepona, evoke for you images of Christ—or as you much prefer, and wisely so, our christic power and yours as well—and Epona, goddess of horses, whom you may not have known before by name except in recesses of your horse-girl memory.

We, Christepona, incorporate for you messages and memories from many: the wisest perspectives and strongest words of some of your most cherished ones who have passed through death. We need now to speak through you, because your world needs to hear us. We include many people and creatures, including some whom you know well.

CHRISTEPONA INTRODUCES HERSELF/THEMSELVES

We meet you through your memory in the voices of Bob and Mary Ann, your parents who personified kindness; Ruth White, who affirmed you as "Reverend" long before anybody else and who, as far as she could, let you in on what it was like, being black in the Jim Crow South; and Betty Smith, your history teacher who told you when you were 15 to trust your voice in a world in which few do.

We reach out to you through your sister priests Sue Hiatt and Alison Cheek, both friends like none other who suffered no fools; your brave bishop Bob DeWitt, and your theological mentor Dorothee Soelle, who together named themselves your "spiritual parents." We come bounding to you through your horse-loving buddy Peg Hall, who left too soon, such a vibrant kindred spirit she was in realms of horses and music and faith.

We approach you here and now in One Spirit of mutual trust and respect. We include many other loved ones, including a coterie of your animal companions. We are here, representing the vast community of saint and sinner spirits swirling through eternity, too many to know or imagine.

We, all of us, need you to speak for all of us. But for some time now, it has been primarily two of us conspiring to spark you to speak in our shared voice.

We are Bev, always close at hand to voice her undying love for you, her courage, her anger at injustice, and her confidence in you; and we are indeed Angela with whom you came to look and see through the veils that divide then and now, here and there.

In ways mysterious to human knowing, including your own, we are converging with others who love you in Christepona. As we two have always done for you, and you for us, we are prying open the doors of your consciousness for others to enter with their confidence in you, their love for you, and their perspectives which, we trust, will comfort and empower you.

And indeed you and your readers, if you believe us, will comfort and empower us as well—because we in the beyond, we in the heavens, we who are leading you eternally, we need your lives to increase our power on your planet, our liberating spirit on the earth.

We need you to speak for us, with us, in our one voice.

TEARS OF CHRISTEPONA

And so we come to you as One—Christepona. Ours is the voice of one G-d of many names. We have come seeking to be heard by you and through you by others. We have come to you because you have long known the difference between, on the one hand, providing a platform, or medium, for someone else's voice and, on the other, being open—vulnerable—to our giving truthful shape to your voice. We know and you know, when you are most honest, that our voice is yours when, but only when, you are most truly aligned with us, and we with one another, and all of us in sacred Spirit. When we are truly aligned in right, mutual relation—it is not an either-or, our voice versus yours. Our voice is one.

If you need an image for this task, think of yourself as our sister and prophet: she who speaks for us and for herself, as one of us, to her people and other creatures, among whom she belongs fully.

A true prophet, unlike those who babble about G-d and Jesus and other precious things, knows well that whatever may befall humankind and creature-kind befalls you as well, and all of us. You and we cannot rise above the fate of the people who choose to turn away, the evildoers, those who live only for themselves. You and we will speak to everyone but only those with ears to hear will know what we are saying, or will care. You and we know sadly that our fate is bound up with the fate of the whole community, including those who ignore us or scorn you. Your heart, like ours, will always be heavy, bearing a burden of joy in who we are and sorrow that so many of our siblings and yours turn away.

And remember: we are not only human and divine. We are other creatures too. You have known this for many years. You have known it in your bones. As you once wrote, Jesus was neither G-d nor un-G-d, but radically both-and. That is true, but you didn't go far enough in your earlier work on mutual relation. You have come to see more clearly over time that our voice is not just human and divine but moreover is the voice of all creatures and creation itself. You, and we, and all human and other creatures, are neither G-d nor are we un-G-d. We are radically both-and, creature and creator—whenever we are

CHRISTEPONA INTRODUCES HERSELF/THEMSELVES

energized through our radical mutuality. And we are energized now, seeking to speak, yearning to be heard.[1]

You know that your waking me to ask me to speak is your answer to my tearful plea—help us!—which I have prayed as a mantra in these stressful times and most immediately in these terribly sad moments of Feather's illness and reliance on me for treatment decisions I haven't known how to make with any confidence. Stumbling along the gravel road at the farm, broken arm in a sling, dear old poodle Bailey bouncing along at my side, trusting me completely in his partial deafness and blindness, and young poodle Joy, full of vigor and mischief, running circles around us. Even in such esteemed company as these two (I am seldom lonely), I have cried out, "Help us!"

We have heard you, and we are here with you, and now it is time for you to speak for yourself—and for us all.

---

1. Readers may find it helpful to know how I hear and pronounce "Christepona." "Christ" has a soft-i (as in the name "Chris" + t). "Epona," a Roman goddess of horses, is pronounced "E-pon-a," accent on "pon." The "e" is soft and the "o" is hard ("e" as in "effort" and "o" as in "pony);" the "a" is soft (as in "art"). In my mind, Christ-epona is pronounced with the accent on "pon": "Christ - e - *pon* - a."

Arrival of COVID-19

But first let's acknowledge that we come through the plants and rocks and the various organic energies—including now the tragedy of coronavirus—to somehow communicate the truth of our interconnectedness globally and universally. We speak as one voice.
Listen!

COVID-19's arrival in the United States as this project was being drawn to a close caused me to reread and rethink what Christepona's voice, vision, wisdom, and tears might mean in the context of the pandemic. The virus made me wonder what Jesus of Nazareth, Mary Ann and Bob Heyward, Beverly Harrison, my horse Feather's mom Red, and the multitude of the souls and spirits of many species, as well as the transcendent spirit connecting us all—the wellspring of Christepona herself—might have to say about our global crisis.

Christepona's perspective on the virus became clear to me as I revisited the draft of the book. During this rereading, her voice became sharper and more compelling to me, perhaps because of the virus. It became clear to me that my job as author was to revise the manuscript as needed to be in sync with Christepona's wisdom, especially on the matter of time.

Yes, it is time for you to begin to see how remarkably nonlinear our time is, Christepona's time. COVID-19 is a virus, and also a teacher. It can teach human beings a great deal about time as gift, opportunity, and resource for better understanding your own lives in time. Feather's myeloma, like your father's and that of many humans who have suffered myeloma, also was triggered by a virus. One of the daunting challenges to contemporary societies around the globe is to learn better how to control these death-dealing viruses—prevent, wherever possible, and mitigate whenever the virus is here already, through medical treatments, currently being researched and tested, and social controls. Science will teach you much of what you'll need to know, but you will only be able to learn spiritual and moral lessons by listening carefully to those whose lives and voices tend to be dismissed as worth little, especially when resources like testing and, eventually, vaccinations, are being distributed.

Here and now, and going forward, it's critical that you realize that, like most illnesses, COVID-19 affects different social classes in different ways—specifically, in this case, in terms of your capacities to maintain social distance as well as your different levels of access to testing and treatment. The deadly unfairness produced by systemic social injustices in general—poverty and racism in particular—makes clear your need as global communities to take strong, sustainable actions to break down economic, class, and racial barriers between and among yourselves. Now is the time.

Yes, many of us have known this all along, but now we know it beyond a shadow of a doubt if we are paying attention to how the coronavirus is impacting different communities throughout the United States and, no doubt we will discover over time, throughout the world.

Christepona's passionate call, throughout these pages, is for us to act collectively and individually to break down our systems of poverty, racism, and other social injustices, and to build up communities of mutual care, justice-love, courage, and radical social transformation in which we humans encourage one another to risk loving one another. Can we do it? Are we able truly to love our neighbors, friend and stranger, alike? Can we empower one another to learn, together, how to love?

Christeopona believes we can, but not without big changes of heart and mind, radical spiritual and social transformation.

Feather and Carter

"It's only a horse—an animal, not a human being." Among humans in the West and throughout the so-called "developed" world, that's the prevailing sentiment. But not only that. In a world of inestimable poverty, unspeakable violence, and terror of all sorts, in which children are starving and tribes are at war and people are dying of wretched diseases including this most recent COVID-19, as well as myeloma, the cancer that afflicts Feather and large numbers of humans, how self-indulgent it is to devote this time and energy to a sick horse that only certain privileged people, usually white, like you, Carter, can afford to have in the first place.

But listen now! To be sure, you and Feather are wrapped in class and race privilege, though not gender privilege, which we'll get to later. Critiquing the importance of your relationship is an exercise in critical thinking, which has its place and is too seldom employed and G-d knows is undervalued in your life together. But right now, to us, it's bullshit and beside the point. You and Feather are above and beyond critical thinking. You are about love and connection, about yourself and a horse who cherishes you. In such Kairos—time beyond time, sacred time—nothing matters more to us, this is Christepona speaking, than the bonding between and among creatures on this earth. We turn to you and Feather to make this point.

Like any two creatures on the planet, human or other, who have forged a mutual relationship, you and Feather experience the yin-yang of up and down, joy and sorrow, often too deep for words. For weeks since you got news of Feather's cancer, we have been wrapping ourselves around you two, to infuse you with our healing powers and bring you peace. We have been attentive to you, listening, day in, *day out. While we hear Feather nibbling her grain and munching her yummy alfalfa hay and while we detect her awareness of some "difference" in routine—no tack and no riding these days—we know Feather is at peace because she's not in pain and her condition is stable right now and because she has her herd close by and because her human family, especially you, are hanging out and paying her lots of attention—grooming, walking, grazing, giving treats. That's how it is for Feather in this moment. She's a bit puzzled, but not afraid. For you, dear Carter, it's not so simple.*

If Feather is dying, I am too. That's what it feels like, and I fall to my knees in tears. The thing about it is, I know it's my despair, not Feather's. She knows no fear of the future, no fear of death. She trusts me. And in this moment, confronted by her cancer, I somehow have to trust Feather to show me the way through my anxiety and my fear for us both, wherever she may be going, I may be going, we may be going.

It's not that Feather has a sweet temperament, because she doesn't in most situations. Like lots of mares, she has an attitude: don't mess with me, unless you're Carter, and if you're Carter, you can mess with me only on the terms we've worked out over our years together.

And we really have worked hard on developing a mutual relationship in which each of us wins and neither of us loses. I enjoy a responsive riding horse as a source of connection and joy, and Feather enjoys being ridden by me and a few others who appreciate her smooth gaits, her athleticism—Feather is a splendid jumper as well as a reliable trail horse—and her willingness to do exactly what her rider asks of her, provided the rider is able to listen to Feather and tune in to her moods and needs.

Because in my ripe older age, having taken up riding only in the last couple of decades, I haven't wanted to do much jumping, and no show jumping, and because Feather loves to jump—a riding instructor named her "Flying Feather"—I was delighted to turn her athletic training over to a couple of much younger women who, for the past several years, until each left to pursue education and employment, enjoyed training Feather, taking her to shows, and winning blue ribbons on their Flying Feather, who was visibly delighted to perform with her young human athletes.

Still, of the various horses we've had since 2000, at our small farm in the North Carolina mountains, Feather is one of the least friendly to passersby and even to those she knows. She's not a schmoozer or talker. She usually doesn't nicker when she sees me coming and she doesn't especially enjoy cozying up to me, much less anyone else. Yet I've learned over the years with Feather, as I also learned with Red, her mom, that Feather values my presence—she'd rather have me with her than somewhere else—and she needs my care and instruction as much as I value hers. Together, exploring nuances of relational mutuality, Feather and I have godded.[1]

Much like Red, whenever Feather is with me, she stands close enough to tune in—though seldom demonstrably—to whatever I am experiencing—joy, sorrow, whimsy, confusion, patience. I can tell because, if my feelings shift or I demonstrate even the slightest change in posture or emotion, Feather notices. She flicks an ear, she glances over at me, she swishes her tail, she shifts her weight toward or away from me. Once in a while, she approaches me and reaches out with her nose to nudge me. Occasionally, but rarely, she nickers. Over the years, Feather and I have learned how to be together, how to stay mutually tuned in, how to regard each other as mighty good pals across the species-line that renders us different characters with needs, temperaments, fears, and expectations that are distinct from each other's as well as from all members of our own species.

So how can I describe what has happened since I discovered that Feather has myeloma, a terminal cancer of the bone marrow, which is terribly rare in horses, and is also a relative of the cancer that killed my father thirty-five years ago?

I can tell you that on October 25, 2019, I felt suddenly as if I also had been stricken with a terminal illness and I wondered, and still do sometimes—against all reason—if Feather and I will somehow die together. I can tell you that I have no desire to die, nor do I actually think I am dying anytime soon, but that I do not want

---

1. Heyward, *Redemption of God*, 163–72.

to live without my precious horse and that everything in me rails against the possibility of losing Feather so much sooner than I had imagined. Like most parents of humans and some other creatures as well, I had always assumed that Feather and I would grow old together—that, in my nineties, I'd be able to sit on my old gray mare, by then in her thirties, and listen to Feather graze, which even now is the sweetest sound in the world to me.

No surprise that a little over a week after I learned of her illness, I fell and broke an arm while visiting her at the vet's barn. Over the next couple of weeks, emerging from debilitating sorrow at least well enough to get back to functioning in my daily life, I began to do frantically what people often do when faced with life-threatening illnesses: researching, researching, and more researching of treatment options of which there are few for this rare equine cancer, and pressing the veterinarians to help me figure out what to do. Over a couple of long, anxiety producing weeks, these competent, caring docs did exactly that. With their guidance, the counsel of loved ones and friends, a few depressing internet reports on equine myeloma, and my own shaky judgment, I opted against a chemo protocol that might or might not have added time to Feather's life but which likely would have seriously diminished the quality of whatever time she may have.

Feather is now home, in our pasture, with me bringing lots of treats, spending time simply standing in the pasture, or paddock, or stall together—Feather and me and usually the other three horses close by, each devoted in their own equine way to Feather and glad enough to have me hanging out almost as one of the herd.

I've taken comfort in realizing that Feather is enjoying her life these days. She has her herd, her grass and hay, she has Velvet the barn cat leaping into her little paddock for company, she has visits from me and, unlike me, Feather is not worried. Taking it a moment at a time, life is good for Feather and, with sadness slipping in around the edges, for me too.

Tenderness and Anger

WE WOULD LOVE TO *be tender in all situations, as we are with Carter and Feather. Through our spirit, we would delight in being able to be tender women and men, tender beings of all kinds, speaking tender words in tender tones, coming across as tender-hearted creatures in tender times—but therein lies the challenge. These times are not tender. These times are angry. We share the anger—specifically at the harm and violence being done to people, other creatures, and the earth itself by those who put themselves at the center of the universe and assume a divine right to boss and bully everyone and everything else, and to concoct whatever lies and tales they can by which to exercise power at whatever cost.*

You are living in crude, ugly, violent times in which tenderness in the public realm is squashed like a bug under indifferent feet. Readers of these words can name a number of those whose tracks are biggest and most dangerous to all living things in this historical moment.

And here we will speak, in an angry finite moment, the name that must be spoken only because the evils he has loosed in America and on planet earth must be acknowledged so that, over time, the good can be restored and deepened structurally, so that economic justice and environmental well-being can be generated in serious, structural ways for the first time. Donald Trump is a morally corrupt, spiritually pathetic human being. Unquestionably, in realms of public perception, he has been your primary collective foil to tenderness since he officially launched his hateful, racist, sexist, xenophobic campaign in 2015. But do not imagine that he is the root problem, because he is not. He is a foul product of a corrupt system that feeds off the poorest and most vulnerable people and creatures on the earth. This perverse economic, white supremacist, and misogynist social system created Trump; he did not create it.

Nonetheless, the effects of Trump's pathological narcissism, his purposeful ignorance of and indifference to the earth and its people near and far, and his megalomaniacal impulses have had a major impact on planetary systems and on all people and creatures. The United States of America and the larger world are in need of some tender rebuilding, because the American people—foolish, frightened, and shortsighted—allowed this man to bully his way into becoming president.

But do not forget, this one man has been merely a representative and pawn of an economic and cultural crisis that has devolved over decades and a couple of centuries into a national and international situation in which ever-more wealth and grandiosity generates ever-more poverty and deprivation, and in which there is little space for tenderness or its twin blessing, kindness, except in the most personal relational arenas of your lives—such as between a woman and her horse—which we in the heavens try to protect from the ruthlessness and cruelty of the public square.

Because Trump has been largely symbolic of deeper historical, social, economic, political, and spiritual problems, and because he himself feeds off of constant attention, good or bad, we hope not to mention him often in these reflections, but rather to consider the conditions around the world that have placed in political power other authoritarian figures in the early decades of the twenty-first century, men such as Putin, Bolsonaro, Orban, Erdogan, Kim, Chi, and Duterte, other men of small soul. Donald Trump is not alone in his hate. But he has the loudest bullhorn on planet earth.

As time goes by, the Trump administration will be tossed into one of American history's garbage heaps and left to rot, but not before significant harm has been done and, we must insist, never to be forgotten. But this is largely up to you and those who follow.

So we speak here not so much tenderly as truthfully—angrily but open to tenderness. Remember that Beverly Wildung Harrison is speaking among us here in Christepona. Her honesty and wisdom, so evident in her great essay, "The Power of Anger in the Work of Love,"[1] infuses our angry voice. Indeed, it is Beverly's voice commanding your attention, here, now, and through eternity.

To realize that Bev—as well as Dorothee, Angela, Alison, Sue, and so many other beloved ones and wise mentors are speaking in your voice—makes my heart sing, Christepona! I have great confidence in their presence and am so very grateful they're speaking collectively with clarity and power. So often one or the other speaks to me as I walk the dogs or groom the horses. Each has always been a truth-speaker who normally refuses to mince words. To have them come together in, as, and through your voice amplifies their wisdom and their collective refusal to be silent in the face of mounting evil.

2021 note: Donald Trump seduced frightened people seeking salvation of one form or another. His evil effect on people has become increasingly evident in the wake of his presidency. His cultish followers remain an ongoing threat to our democratic republic. The forces that put him in the White House and kept him there for four years—a combination of corporate wealth, bizarre conspiracy theories, and Trump's own construction of an empire built on lies and hateful assaults—continue to mount death-dealing threats to American democracy and to the most racially, economically, environmentally, and sexually vulnerable among us. If anything, the urgency of Christepona's voice is greater today than ever.

---

1. Harrison, "Power of Anger," 3–21.

Time Is Up

THE TIME IS UP *for mincing words in the United States of America. It is simply not okay to have avowed white supremacists shaping public policy near your highest seats of power. Nor is it morally acceptable to have an unregulated capitalist economic system rendering increasing numbers of children hungry when they arrive at school even in a land of plenty, but plenty for whom? Shame! Shame on those who believe that it is anything but evil to kill people for oil or land or to generate ever-more profit for the wealthiest among you, humanitarian costs be damned. How in G-d's name can you act as if it's within the contestable range of normal democracy to tolerate big men in business, entertainment, and government for whom lying is a way of life; entitlement to wealth a personal privilege; abuse of power a weapon of choice; and the use and abuse of women a way to pleasure themselves without consequences?*

The time is up for hesitating to name evil when you see it. There may be no concentration camps, but what are those cages and tents at your southern border? Most United States citizens think of yourselves as loving, welcoming people. So how do you square your national hospitality with the bans against Mexicans and Muslims entering your country, or with the bashing of poor black and brown people from "shithole" countries like Somalia and Haiti, and the wide-scale incarceration of so many youth of color and the shooting deaths of so many people for simply walking while black down the street?

Whether or not you name it as such, it's evil, and it's on you.

You, the people of the United States, are responsible for this moral corruption, and the time is up for your collusion through silence or equivocation.

In your moral conundrum, you have learned to expect that many of the highest officials in executive, legislative, and judicial branches of your federal government will simply lie, make up reality, offer "alternate facts" whenever it suits them, about anything. The time is up for you to simply shake your heads and go about washing the dishes, walking the dogs, and watching progressive cable news, where you learn from and agree with bold journalists like Rachel Maddow, who've done their homework and attempt to analyze the news honestly, intelligently, and fairly, usually raising more questions than providing answers, which is what good journalists do.

In your current situation, you cannot depend on your churches, temples, mosques, covens, and other religious organizations to specify the abuses of power as morally indefensible and as requiring you to speak and act. So what are you waiting for, you who consider yourselves moral, or spiritual, persons and who share responsibility for contending against the forces of evil in your midst?

Let us be clear. We, Christepona, know, as you know, that you are being lied to constantly by men and women who have cast their lots with the richest of the rich. So what are you going to do about it? There is no moral excuse for apathy in this evil situation. None. The time is up for you to say nothing and do even less.

Most of you know that the safety and well-being of most Americans, indeed most creatures on this planet, are at stake: poor people; black, brown, and other people of color; women of all colors; LGBTQ people; people of minority faith or spiritual traditions; millions of people locked up for nonviolent and often no crimes at all; people who are sick, old, handicapped, overdosing on opioids pedaled for profit, and otherwise especially vulnerable people and creatures.

You know this, but what will you say, and to whom, and how uncompromisingly?

It is time to leave your living rooms and kitchens, your offices and farms, your studios and classrooms, and join the movements for justice, compassion, sanity, and peace. In the ongoing crisis of

COVID-19, you may have to come together in cyber rooms, through social media, honest conversations with neighbors and friends, written communications, phone calls, and small group gatherings. Wherever, whenever, and however you can, it's time for your best selves to speak out, come together, and change the world.

Many Americans and others around the world know for a fact that, as the earth suffers, you are being led toward the abyss by climate change–deniers who are blinded by the glint of the almighty silver dollar. You know this for sure, but what actions are you willing to take to stem the toxic tides? It is time for you to come together and join forces with people who are fighting to save the planet.

You have been horrified by images of children being ripped from their parents' arms at the border. You recoiled at the photograph of Oscar Alberto Martinez and his not-yet two-year old daughter, Angie Valeria, lying face down, drowned in the Rio Grande. But what did you do with your horror other than swallow it or share it in the safe spaces of your own lives? It is time to come out of your safe spaces, and come together. Together, united in one voice, united with us, you and we can stem these evil tides.

We, Christepona, are urging you to join us. Now. Do not be put off by our anger. Share it. Share our anger. It's not at you personally but at the state of affairs in America and on planet earth that calls for you to be involved, with us, now and eternally.

Moving beyond the madness of one United States president, we ask you to speak the truth publicly and collectively, demonstrating the best of your political and religious practices, those steeped universally in traditions of moral courage. Do not be onlookers! Speak and act, pool your talents and resources to make a difference, however small it may seem to you. Believe us, it is never too small when you are speaking and acting for justice and compassion.

And now the coronavirus is working its way among animals and humans and confounding the whole inhabited earth. As we speak, many of you who can be are at home, seeking safety, if possible, for yourselves and others. But let us say it again: Being in your homes doesn't make it less urgent to speak up. The time has come for you to let your voices be heard however you can—virtually, and in other individual and collective ways, resurrecting such good old tried and tested tactics as phoning and letter writing as well as on some of the current organizing platforms.

It is no time to worry about who might be offended by anything you say.

No time to refrain from speaking the truth as boldly as you can.

No time to fret about being misunderstood.

No time to make nice.

Time is up.

I hear you, sisters, brothers, siblings, fellow creatures, Christepona, and I'm heartened by your encouragement for us to come together and speak truth to power without worrying about whether we're stepping beyond our colleagues and friends who don't want to risk alienating those still standing in the middle, afraid to move too far to the left, hesitant to be seen as feminist or socialist or secular or un-American. Sometimes, though not much recently, this has been me, trying so hard to reach out to the middle that I don't connect clearly with the boldest truth-speakers, even though I am often among them myself—always among them when in your company, Christepona. Please tell us what we need to hear and literally encourage us to speak and act.

2021 note: It's clear that this is a moment to speak and act boldly. President Joe Biden urges unity, a positive vision of possibility, but we are far from any real unity in the United States. Working for and insisting on weaving justice-love into the fabric of our society's foundation must be our priority, relentlessly, uncompromisingly. Over time, our unity will be woven out of our shared work for justice and common well-being.

Time and Eternity

VERY WELL. WE BEGIN in kairos *(Greek for "eternity")*, *not in time as you normally experience it. Our voice rises from another time zone as it were, a time not measured by human calendars and clocks. The presence of another dimension of time, beyond your clocks and calendars, has been made more acute for many of you during the COVID crisis. Consider the possibility that you are, in some mysterious ways, living in a time beyond time; that you are being tugged beyond the linear confines of "keeping time" that have become so familiar to most of you. Could this be so?*

Before COVID arrived, Christepona had talked with me about *kairos* and *chronos* as a way of lifting up and exploring the intermingling of our human experiences of time as we most often refer to it and another dimension of time that draws us not simply above and beyond, but more deeply within, beneath, through, and around the time we keep via clocks and schedules. Christepona suggests that the coronavirus may have pulled us collectively more consciously into *kairos.*

*Let us be clear that this extraordinary time—*kairos*—does not refer to an "afterlife" about which many of you may have doubts or at least honest questions. The* kairos *or eternity in which we speak and write is here and now, infusing your lives today in the world of* chronos *(Greek for the linear chronological time you keep via schedules and day-timers). Our* kairos *is transforming your* chronos *into a spiritual platform for deeper, broader, more far-reaching experiences of what is going on and of who you are.*

To believe that you are living in kairos *requires a leap of faith, not necessarily Christian faith. As a matter of historic fact, most Christian orthodoxy—"right thinking" Christianity—has conceptualized "eternity" as a realm either entirely above or wholly beyond the world. The Christian church has painted a picture of kairos or eternity as "heaven," a realm above and beyond your life on earth—and there for you only if you have been "good." Think of Saint Nicholas, Santa Claus, rewarding good children. That's pretty much the way traditional Christianity has imaged G-d in relation to his children's behavior.*

In chronos, most Christians and practitioners of other patriarchal religions on the planet have either persecuted or idealized those who share our knowledge of kairos as a realm of time that is here and now. Such mystics, because that's what we are, are usually portrayed as heretics or crazy or else they are set apart as saints. We are mystics—people and creatures involved in the mysteries of kairos. Perhaps we are also saints, perhaps we are heretics or crazy or just plain old commonfolk and creatures who have died, yet who live on through you, in whom we breathe and act and speak. Whatever, we are bearers of the Spirit that many Christians call G-d. And while we are mystics, we live and move around in the world in and through regular folks—like the writer and readers of this book—who believe they and others are often touched and empowered by the sacred Spirit who names herself and themselves in these pages as Christepona. Consider the possibility that you too are mystics.

More than most Christian leaders over time, mystics like Hildegard de Bingen (1098-1179), Julian of Norwich (1342-c. 1416), and Thomas Merton (1915-1968), and imaginative fiction writers like Charles Williams (1886-1945), Madeleine L'Engle (1918-2007), Octavia Butler (1947-2006) and J. K. Rowling (b. 1965) have brilliantly conveyed intimations of kairos in their work.

Our primary motive for speaking and needing to be heard on this matter of time and eternity is that we know so well that chronological time is slipping away from your nations and from the earth, as well as from each of you personally. Those of you on the short side of life, which is most who have lived at least 50 chronological calendar years, are increasingly aware that this is so.

The earth is undergoing significant disruption and devastation due to climate change that is damaging and eventually will destroy its waters, soil, and sky and its creature-kind, human and other. The tragedies are already abundant. Witness in the early part of 2020 the days of red sky and terrified creatures in southeast Australia. Witness throughout the earliest days of this century the draughts and famines driving people north from Africa, across the Mediterranean, at great risk and often death, seeking refuge in some safer place on earth, which the map identifies as Europe.

Witness here and now, as this book draws toward completion, the arrival of the coronavirus, one of a chain of kindred viruses, spreading among creatures of different species, who share life and death processes. These processes are infused with toxins and destructive energies that largely reflect your human indifference to the energies of life and death on your planet home.

This is the context in which we urge you to think about time— chronos *and* kairos—*in a critical moment of your history, your time, your* chronos. *You live your days in chronological order. You set your clocks so you will know what time it is. You keep time. You measure time, you lose time or you gain it, you have time or you don't, you're on time or you're late. You experience time as a commodity, like food or clothing, something you buy if you can, but eventually you run out of time. This happens as you move closer to death, which is every one of you, individuals who are aging, and as a planet suffering from humanity's collective ignorance and indifference, intentional disregard, and willful plundering.* Chronos *is the time you eventually will have no more of, the time that is slipping away from you. Like water through the fingers, your* chronos *is running out.*

Buying Time?

But oh! The loss of time, the loss of chronos, is what humans in the West are conditioned to deny. Individually, many humans with economic resources turn away from aging and death by covering up the lines of time, coloring over their greying hair, and running, jumping, stretching, hopping, bouncing, and moving around as much as they can to keep their bodies feeling less time-bound. Witness all the jogging on beaches and along paths in urban parks by people of diverse genders, ages, cultures, and colors, people buying time.

Collectively, you refuse to accept that you are running out of time. You are so conditioned, through your political economy, to buying your way out of crises that you can't imagine any problems—global crises of climate change, draught, starvation, fire, flood, or viruses—that are too big for the experts to solve with money and a little more time. Perhaps you also pray, depending on how you may experience the roles of our spirits and sacred Source in relation to your experiences of major crises.

And so those with resources buy time and also votes to keep political power in the hands of those who deny not only climate change but also the passing away of their time on this earth as a species. These climate change deniers, and their political proxies, are fools living in fantasy land, even as they jog the time away on treadmills in five-star hotels where they plot to keep people in power to protect their profits. As for the well-being of others? On behalf largely of themselves, these very rich men and occasionally women, who are mostly white, insist that all reports of the earth being in danger are overblown, exaggerated, or in any case are not to be taken seriously when what seems to be at stake is the almighty dollar.

These truth-deniers have learned that buying time is a luxury of wealth and social privilege, and that it works, at least for a while longer. And it does work for them, until someday when it doesn't. Because regardless of who they are and no matter how attached they may be to their privileges, their wealth and their power, their lifestyles and their opinions, and even perhaps to planet earth as a place for their own enjoyment, their time is slipping away, and soon it will be up.

So this is one reason for our speaking now, while you still have some time. Your chronos is important, because every minute you have together as siblings to forge mutuality with your planet and one another is precious time. Every act of kindness you receive or give is a moment in time to change lives. Every time you are able to experience yourselves together in mutually caring ways and to generate joy and gratitude is time well spent, always a mingling of chronos and kairos, time as you measure it and time beyond time, an eternity you share with us in hints and intimations.

So let's go a little further in considering this kairos, which is visible through the eyes of faith. When transformed by kairos, chronos, plain old chronological time, the kind that tick tocks round the clock, no longer runs vertically in a line from past through present toward future. When touched by kairos, your chronos also becomes more interesting. As your experiences of time begin to spin and spiral, you realize that your past and your future are both alive in the present.

Case in point. While you may dismiss or denounce this, it has been the experience of many people who use so-called "psychedelic" drugs that the earth's natural hallucinogens can sharpen their senses of kairos. These drugs have been used not just over the past few decades in the West, but through ages of mystical practices, often among native peoples around the planet, living close to the earth and aware of what it has to offer.

But, of course, we must say to you that even natural psychedelics can be dangerous to those not practiced in using them reverently and wisely, which is most people in the West whose spiritualities are disconnected from nature and earth. Such practice can be learned only with *great purpose and care over lifetimes and generations of mentoring by ancestors and wise ones, not in weekend retreats.*

So let us say something that is far more important—probably for most of you, and certainly for Carter, herself an addict—without such stimulants as peyote or marijuana, but simply through faith and prayer, you can spiral in your experiences of time and space rather than simply walking a straight line from past to future and from here to there. You can glimpse the future in the present and know that your past is living in you and working through you here and now. You will see that the past is never past and that the future is always involved with you here and now. You will know you are always becoming. You will not need drug-induced visions to realize, simply through your faith, the power and presence of eternity with and in you here and now.

You will see that whatever is most beautiful, truthful, and kind, whatever is wisest and most fully mutual, among you humans and other creatures, originates in kairos *and lives far beyond your measured lives here on earth. This means that anything in this book with lasting value, any word or sentiment, any paragraph or passage, that conveys love, wisdom, or truth, is a gift from Christepona and is rooted in* kairos, *eternity.*

We ourselves—Christepona—are a gift from eternity, a gift of kairos.

And the most basic thing for you to remember, which bears repeating, is that eternity does not refer to "heaven" or to an "afterlife" as these notions have been constructed within traditional Christianities as prizes for right thinking or right behavior. Eternity is not a prize or a lure. It is a moment of intimate involvement with the Sacred—generating justice-love, mutuality, empathy, kindness, compassion, courage, and many other relational gifts, in your everyday lives as individuals and communities.

You experience eternity on earth, because your lives are wrapped in it. What you normally experience as time moves you along in kairos *can be imagined as a larger time beyond your capacities even to imagine. As twentieth century Christian theologian Paul Tillich tried to image a "G-d beyond G-d," we are speaking to you here of a "time beyond time," which can only be imagined as truly unimaginable. Your way to* kairos *is only through faith, an open mind, a yearning heart, and an active imagination.*[1]

In your chronological lives, you are cradled by eternity. In this same way, whatever you say and do that may evoke empathy or kindness, truth or wisdom, and whoever you may be—you who are writing, reading, and reflecting in this moment—your words and the meanings you find here, if they enhance your humanity and contribute to the wisdom of creation, are steeped in kairos.

So we continue where we began, here and now, in kairos, *inviting you to take this liminal leap with us beyond the routines, some important, some trivial, of what you have become accustomed to as passing time.*

It's hard to grasp the radicality of your words, Christepona, the transformative power of what it would mean to join you consciously in *kairos*, to step with you intentionally beyond time as we are accustomed to keeping it, and really experience our past, present, and future as all rolled into one eternal moment of resisting evil by loving our neighbors, loving the world, and loving ourselves boldly, without apology.

Do we, dear readers, grasp the revolutionary character of Christepona's invitation? It is, I believe, the same revolutionary call of Jesus and of all true prophets of the Spirit of Justice-Love, whose voices merge in Christepona.

---

1. Tillich, *Systematic Theology*, vol. 2, 369–62.

Mutuality: The Core of Goodness/God/Godding

We now come to the heart of morality and of everything we are hoping to convey. We need to consider the soulful work of discerning good and evil, because most if not all spiritual reflections, moral questions, political activities, and very often our tears, lead to this pivotal task of moral discernment. Indeed, all matters of conscience, conviction, and commitment live in tension between good and evil and derivative questions about right and wrong.

Your concepts of good and evil provide the moral foundations of your life together as human beings and social creatures by shaping the ethical contours of your understandings of right and wrong.

From early in your work, in The Redemption of God *(1982), you began to use the word "god" as a verb—suggesting that humans can "god" together. This was and still is a radical proposal in which your theological understanding of G-d or "godding" and your ethical understanding of what is good, or goodness, are synonymous, are they not?*

Yes, that's correct. For at least forty years, I've understood God as our power to generate right, mutual relation—what is always good—in our life together. I would say that when we "god," or when we "love"—these are synonymous—we make God incarnate. This is always good.

This is radical, and especially important, because you are proposing that, in your choices—for good or evil—human beings not only affirm or reject G-d. You actually embody *the spirit of G-d.*

MUTUALITY: THE CORE OF GOODNESS/GOD/GODDING

You either "god" or you fall toward or into evil, participating in and perpetuating attitudes, acts, and structures of evil.

All religious traditions and people have ways of understanding good and evil. Concepts of good and evil, together with right and wrong, are common to all cultures and societies, regardless of whether there is any explicit concept of G-d, or any religion. These ethical base-points transcend national and religious boundaries and they vary from one time and place to another. Each culture, religion, social institution, or historical period reflects its own particular understandings of good and evil and, from there, its own rules and customs about right and wrong attitudes (what you think) and behavior (how you act). Particular understandings of good and evil do not spring out of nowhere but have roots either in long-standing traditions and assumptions or they are born as new awareness and greater knowledge work to reform your moral foundations.

Let me continue, Christepona, to say what I mean by these terms—good and evil—not that my understanding is either unique or best, but that it is something, as you have noted, that I have worked on, as a theologian and simply as a person, for decades. My roots are in overlapping Western and Christian traditions. In fact, these roots are not unique to the Christian West. "Mutuality," a term which I borrow from the Jewish social philosopher Martin Buber, is key to our morality.

Mutuality has even deeper roots in spiritual and cultural traditions that predate both Christianity and modern Euro-American cultures. Still it is important, because it is most honest, for me to acknowledge my own Christian and Western moral foundations. For only if I, and we, can be reasonably knowledgeable of our sources, and as honest as possible in stating what we believe about good and evil, can anything else we say in these pages be intelligible or trustworthy.

"Good" and "evil" are moral constructs, which means they pertain primarily to human actions and attitudes, not so much to the behavior of other creatures, animals, or plants, although cases can be made for the good and evil activities of other species. Without wishing to limit ourselves to humanity's life on this planet, we are concerned in these pages, primarily although not necessarily or exclusively, with morality as a human category of discerning what is good and what is evil and of doing our best to act on behalf of the good, or God.

With this in mind, I affirm that whatever is "good," or whatever is God, generates greater mutuality—that is, more God—and that whatever is "evil" shatters possibilities for building or sustaining mutual relation. We believe that good and evil refer to the moral character of relationship in both smaller (personal, interpersonal) and larger (organizational, societal, national, global) arenas of our lives.

We are "good" to the extent that we are related, connected, in such a way that our relationship generates greater mutuality. Whether as individuals or as different groups, families, communities, nations, cultures, religions—and more than most of us realize, also as species—our mutuality is a quality of connectedness through which each or all of us are empowered to be ourselves at our best, living fully into our own special talents, aspirations, needs, and capacities for productivity and joy.

If our relationship is truly mutual, we spark creativity in one another's lives. Both or all of us are empowered in some ways to be most truly who we are capable of being. For example, as a teacher, I evoke your best and, as a student, you elicit mine. We may be parents and children, doctors and patients, musicians, artists, fellow workers and colleagues of similar or different ranks. We may be spouses, partners, lovers, friends. In larger arenas, we may be allied or estranged nations or religions. We may be different species of plants or animals. We may be individuals or groups still relatively unknown to each other who can help rather than hinder one another along the way. To the extent that our relationships encourage one another to be ourselves as fully, productively, and joyfully as possible, we are generating more mutuality—and it is good. We are godding.

Evil

YES, AND EVIL IS *whatever breaks mutuality into pieces of blame, acrimony, and alienation. Let us speak frankly about how evil looks to us, from the perspective of eternity:*

Evil diminishes and eventually destroys your human capacities, and even your desire, for mutuality. Evil is rooted in your fear of not having enough of something—money, food, water, power, sexual or economic control. In fear, you strive for more and more of whatever it is until even a vague and distant dream of mutual relation disappears. You are driven to protect yourselves from those who want what you assume is yours to be taken, owned, and guarded rather than shared.

The well-being of others, except some whom you may know and care about personally, recedes from your concerns. Fearing that you will be losers, let down, or left out, your attitudes and controlling behavior generate evil both in your daily lives and in the larger realm of your common life.

None of you is a stranger to fear and all of you have had some role in perpetuating the evils that have been structured historically into your common life: The genocide perpetrated against native peoples and the economic institution of slavery are massive evils woven over time into the moral fabric of your societies. In America, the evil of white supremacy has spawned more suffering than even the most passionately anti-racist among you can realize—slaughtering native and black and brown and Asian people, lynching, raping, segregating, Jim Crow, mass incarceration, voter suppression, the list goes on. By terrorizing people of all races and cultures, both dominant and subordinate, evil holds on.

This is why so many white people in the United States have reacted to the murder of young black men by police and to the reemergence of the Black Lives Matter movement as a threat against white people rather than as a liberating call to all people and to your entire society. This is an example of evil's tenacity to keep twisting human attitudes and behavior long after its initial savaging of your societies through genocide and slavery.

Out of your histories emerges ongoing tension between good and evil. On the one hand, there are always struggles around the world to create more fully mutual societies, in which generating justice-love is a common goal. On the other hand, reactionary efforts are ongoing by those determined to thwart all moral and political efforts to secure mutuality as a social foundation. Morally ignorant or indifferent, spiritually apathetic, and politically reactionary people mock and trivialize the dreams of a good society, secured by structures that promote mutuality.

The tensions between good and evil are constant and ubiquitous not only in white supremacist, global capitalist, and misogynist societies around the world but in all cultures, societies, and subcultures here, there, and everywhere, because none of you, and none of your societies, lives beyond the ongoing challenges of moral discernment.

Hear, Hear, Christepona! Many people on the planet who share some version of a spirituality of mutuality are angered by the ugly, violent, morally bankrupt efforts of bombastic political leaders, manipulated by economic high stakeholders, fear-based and driven by greed, to trample in the dust most of what is potentially good and radically mutual on this earth. We who are here on this planet right now are facing many moral challenges, and our work is simultaneously spiritual and political, economic and cultural. Humans will always have to contend with evil. But this time, right now, is our time.

Christofascism

2021 note: What follows here, in Christepona's voice, is every bit as relevant, and at least as important, today as when Trump was in office.

You are right about that, Carter. Arriving in kairos, we woke you up and urged you to speak for us for two reasons:

First, we wanted to place the tender relationship between you and Feather in a larger context so as to illuminate the transformative power of mutuality and love as a mighty spiritual resource in the struggle against the hate-filled injustice, cruelty, and violence with which much of humankind and creature-kind has to cope. We lift up your and Feather's bond to exemplify the power of personal relationships everywhere in the world, the power of relationships through which justice-workers, activists, mentors, healers, liberators, spiritual leaders, moral teachers, and other concerned humans draw strength for the struggle.

Second, we are compelled to name the political present in the United States and elsewhere today on planet earth as fascist—most terribly as "christofascist," fascism being mounted in the name of Christ, as one of us, Dorothee Soelle, once named the dreadful authoritarian, nationalistic, racist, sexist, xenophobic, profit-driven power grab by ruthless—for the most part—white affluent men.

Through Dorothee, we introduced the term "christofascism" to students and faculty at the Union Theological Seminary in New York City sometime in the 1980s.[1] *Dorothee's point of reference was the*

---

1. I don't recall exactly when I first heard Dorothee Soelle speak of "christofascism." Nor do I recall reading it in her work. I do remember several

economic and militaristic platform of Ronald Reagan, who had been inaugurated president of the United States in 1981. Dorothee Soelle sensed where America might be headed—and where you are indeed headed half a century later.

What did Dorothee see that reminded her of events in her native Germany in the mid-twentieth century?

Did she notice similarities between the social anxieties that motivated Germans and Americans to hand over the reins of economic and cultural power-shaping to populist candidates with untrustworthy moral moorings?

Did she notice the passive, apolitical roles of most mainstream Christian churches in the two national cultures? Did she imagine that clergy and other religious leaders in the United States would not resist the oppressive policies of authoritarian national leadership any more than the German Christian churches had resisted Hitler?

Did Dorothee notice, more than anything else, that the "America First" slogans of Reagan and his administration were a throwback to the Third Reich's obsession with itself as the greatest—eventually the only great—nation on earth?

Did she fear that Hitler's anti-Semitism, steeped in his raising up of the "Aryan race," was reemerging in the Reagan administration's focus on law and order, the punishment of social dissidents and minorities, a renewed heralding of white men's rights and privileges in American society, and the emergence of a "Moral Majority" of reactive white male Christian leadership in close conversation with the Reagan government?

Dorothee Soelle taught Christian theology and wrote poetry for over forty years until her death in 2003. Based part-time in New York City and much of the time in her native Hamburg, she traveled the world as an advocate for social justice and for building a world without war.

---

conversations with her at Union Theological Seminary, or maybe at one of the retreats we led together, in which she furrowed her brow and was clearly troubled as she reflected on the "christofascism" she saw creeping into the United States in the early days of the Reagan administration, in the early 1980s. It was an unforgettable term then and now.

Dorothee Soelle was intensely focused on combatting the distortions of Christian spirituality that supported the trickle-down economic policy being put in place by Reagan. This distortion, which her colleague and close friend Beverly Harrison later would call "capitalist spirituality," was heresy to Dorothee. Likewise, she saw the United States' covert assaults on small neighbors like Grenada and Nicaragua not only as unnecessary and violent but moreover as moral travesties, evil events, with ominous historical precedence in the Third Reich.

She interpreted the economic and militaristic policies that took hold during the Reagan administration, and which were strengthened through the support of Christianity's Moral Majority, as the reemergence of christofascism—an authoritarian, white supremacist, misogynist, xenophobic, economically exploitative regime strengthened by the peddling of the Christian heresy that puts individual self-interest at the center of all that is good.

Dorothee Soelle had prayed that such fascism had been defeated in 1945 but, by the mid-1980s, especially in the United States, she lamented what she feared was growing on the planet. In the almost twenty years since her death, Soelle's warning of the rise of christofascism among you has been born out. Despite, or perhaps because of, the election in 2008 of Barack Obama as president, the racist character of fascism has surfaced with vitriol in the United States.

Building, moreover, on the legacy of Reagan's preference for unregulated capitalism and the wealth it generates for multinational corporations controlled largely by white men, the United States has become over four decades a country in which increasing numbers of workers and poor people, white, black, brown, Native, and Asian, have been unable to secure ample resources for life—food, shelter, health care, and good education.

Through dynamics of structural poverty, white supremacy, and misogyny, the United States had been readying itself unaware for the rise of another populist president in 2016, thirty-six years after the election of Ronald Reagan. Of course, the president of the United States is by no means the only authoritarian leader that has been recently elected or installed around the world as hyper-nationalist—racist, sexist, heterosexist, anti-immigrant, xenophobic, and hostile to the environment. Christofascists like Duterte of the Philippines and Bolsonaro of Brazil have become allies to nativist leaders of Russia, China, North Korea, Saudi Arabia, Turkey, Israel—and the United States.

So what then is your work in this christofascist situation?

In the iconic words of labor organizer Mother Jones (1837 to 1930), you must pray for the dead and fight like hell for the living. Your shared spiritual task and political charge in these times is to speak out against injustice and oppression in all forms—and to support in whatever ways you can those siblings struggling for justice and liberation everywhere, trusting yourselves and those whose values you share and whose lives you trust to come together in transforming the societies in which you live.

Don't say there's nothing you can do, because that's a lie. Don't fool yourselves. You can pay attention and get informed. Speak out. Write. Preach. Sing. Make music or drama or art. Share stories. Listen. Join groups that promote your values. Give money as you can. Pray and pray some more, which is what you're doing if you're listening to us now.

The revolution is never won and your goals and aspirations will never be fully realized. But do not give up, not now, not ever. Do whatever you can, do it together and, step by step, often only by the smallest steps, you will move the struggle toward brighter days not just for yourselves but for all humans and other creatures.

In all probability, you—the author and readers of this book—will not see many of the fruits of your own labor. You yourselves are not likely to see much light at the end of the dark tunnels through which you are moving right now. But your work will bear fruit for those who are coming along to harvest, and your wrestling through the darkness toward the light that beckons you will enable younger ones to grow up in more justice-affirming communities in a world being made new, thanks to your efforts and your faith.

In all movements for social justice, including the recurrent struggles against fascism, some people—prophets and radicals—will be on the leading edges of social transformation. Some people will form the middle, forging compromises and strategies by which your battles will be well designed and clever. Some of you will bring up the rear, perhaps slower to emerge in the movements for justice, but strong and tenacious in backing up those who lead the way, positioning yourselves to help secure longer-term social change.

It is imperative that you understand that all movements for social justice have people in each of these positions in the struggles—leading, following, holding the middle—with many of you moving back and forth among these roles, as situations require.

Believe us, because we know, we who are Christepona. We know because we have been there. You must respect, not resent, one another's roles. And you must play your own as well as you can. Wherever in the struggles you find yourselves, or are placed by time and circumstance, act with as much integrity, intelligence, skill, and patience as you can. Now.

Oh friends, I can underscore from my own life and work in church, seminary, and various justice movements what Christepona is stressing here about the urgency for us to play different roles in the struggles against fascism here and now. Sure, once upon a time, as younger people, with more energy and greater access to public platforms, any of us might have been leaders in these struggles on a larger stage. I might have been, you might have been, and perhaps even now some of you are or some of you will be, someday.

Today I'm grateful to be a smaller player on a mountain top in North Carolina, active in local justice movements, happy to live among other justice-loving, progressive humans, most with animal friends of various species, and active as a Christian, still an Episcopal priest, in a local Unitarian Universalist congregation. These days I'm usually in the middle-line of the fight for justice-love—seldom at the vanguard, seldom at the rear. I'm glad to imagine stepping forward or back, as needed, as we go forward together. I wonder where others of you may see yourselves in our ongoing struggles for justice, liberation, and social healing, our struggles against the fascism that threatens to undo all that is good and just.

Justice-love: Beyond Sentiment

THE WORD "LOVE" IS *often used as a sentiment, signaling personal feelings of attraction or attachment of one form or another. But real love—justice-love—is G-d. And justice-love, or G-d, is revolutionary action on behalf of liberation and healing in the world, near at hand and far away. Revolutionary love does not require guns, bombs, or other weapons of violence. Revolutionary love creates not only justice—right, mutual relation; it also generates acts and attitudes of compassion, kindness, and forgiveness as, together, people strive to rebuild the world around them, between them, within them.*

Stop imagining that love is simply about your personal relationships, being in love, cherishing your partners, friends, children, and animal companions; simply about weddings and birthday parties and celebrations of those whom you love. These events and relationships are wonderful and they are truly loving when they embody mutual joy between people, and even more so when they celebrate a larger community of support and need. In many weddings and other personal celebrations, people lift up their shared recognition that humans and creatures of all kinds are important to them, because they realize that their relationships, marriages, and partnerships can thrive only through one another's kindness, generosity, and shared advocacy for justice for all people and creatures, stretching out beyond themselves to generate justice-love for their neighbors as well as themselves.

True love means doing your part, in the prophet Micah's words, to make justice roll down like waters and righteousness like

JUSTICE-LOVE: BEYOND SENTIMENT

an ever-flowing stream.[1] *This is why it was proposed in the last part of the twentieth century by a group of Presbyterian liberation theologians, including Marvin Ellison and Sylvia Thorson-Smith, that "love" more truthfully is "justice-love"*[2]—*designated by a single, hyphenated, English word to denote a single act and movement among us. Justice-love.*

It is simply a fact that love without justice is not love at all, but only a sentiment, a sweet feeling. It is also true that justice has little staying power without love at its core, because love is the active, ongoing motive to create justice as right, mutual relation. This mutuality is the revolutionary basis of all good relationships, social institutions, and political movements. Nothing either loving or just will ever be built through violence, torture, lies, or contempt for your adversaries.

Justice-love is the moral cornerstone of your common life. As your staying power, justice-love is built on the relational dynamic of mutuality, through which all parties are healed or liberated in ways they can experience, affirm, and celebrate. A justice-loving marriage is built on dynamics of mutuality and frees both people in ways they may not have realized they needed. A marriage built on emotions or expressions of "love" that are not just—violence, control, lies—will not contribute over the long run to the joy and happiness of any relationship.

Wherever there is commitment to building justice-love—in marriage, family, or government; in friendship, school, or religion; in professional, social, or political situations—the possibilities for joy and well-being are greatly increased. The health of the family, community, institution, or movement is strengthened immeasurably. Dynamics of relational mutuality hold the key to releasing your better angels in every situation. The greater the mutuality of all who are involved, the more effective—loving, just, and productive—your relationships, families, organizations, movements. By contrast, the stronger the dynamics of control and domination by key figures, the less productive and healthy your relationships,

---

1. Micah 6:8
2. Ellison and Thorson-Smith, *Body and Soul.*

families, and communities over time, and the more inevitably turbulent and sorrowful.

What then are some essential components in building dynamics of mutuality, securing structures of justice-love, and struggling effectively against the rise of christofascism in smaller and larger arenas of your life together?

Empathy, Kindness, Compassion, and Courage

WHEREVER YOU POSITION YOURSELVES *in the struggles against contemporary fascism, you will be involved in generating dynamics of mutuality, which will contribute to the building or securing of structures of justice-love in large and small places among yourselves. Your moral work as creatures in this struggle depends on your capacities to experience empathy, practice kindness, show compassion, and keep your courage, the strongest moral roots of your common humanity.*

You might think of these capacities as quadruplet spirits— qualities born together in your hearts, minds, and souls; qualities that go together and are never far apart in your life. Empathy, kindness, compassion, and courage constitute a moral compass to keep you on the way of your true humanity, creatureliness, and participation with us in divinity. Embodying these qualities, you remember who you are. As moral beacons, your empathy, kindness, compassion, and courage focus an intense laser beam on the best options available to you in every choice you make between right and wrong, decisions you make daily, again and again. Together, these capacities enable you to god.

Empathy is your capacity to know deep in your heart, mind, and bones what someone else is experiencing and, to some extent, to share the other's joy or sorrow, suffering or pleasure. The opposite of empathy is apathy, an unwillingness to suffer with another and therefore a shutting down of any capacity to really know someone else.

Kindness is how you express empathy. It's an expression of connection and tenderness with a sister-brother-sibling human or creature. The opposite of kindness is callousness, cruelty, indifference, either actively hurting or turning away from another.

Compassion is empathic kindness extended into situations in which some wrong has been done. In such situations, in which someone has been hurt, compassion is a potentially transformative moral response to those who have been hurt as well as to those who have inflicted the harm. The opposites of compassion are apathy or contempt, a refusal to get involved or an insistence on retribution, vengeance, or harsh, cruel punishment.

Courage is the moral energy that rises from the heart and moves you to stand on behalf of whatever is most empathic, kindest, and most compassionate in any situation in which you find yourselves. Courage has nothing to do with not being afraid, because you are often afraid of many things, some of which you should be. To keep your courage is—despite your fear—to practice empathy, kindness, and compassion.

Without empathy, kindness, compassion, and courage, sooner or later, you will hate your neighbors. This is because your "human nature" enables you to both love and hate. You are not "naturally" either good or evil, but rather are able to be either or both, depending on the situations in which you find yourselves. It certainly can, and often does, seem more natural, more like who you are, and more like what you feel, to hate those who are themselves so hateful of the most vulnerable among you humans and other creatures on the earth.

Without these moral capacities, these beacons to illuminate your way, you are likely to fall into hating humanity, hating your siblings, and eventually hating yourselves as well. This moral devolution will shrink you spiritually, sap your soul, and leave you miserable, even though you may appear to be successful, glamorous, and powerful, as some of the world's most pitiful leaders appear to be.

With empathy, kindness, compassion, and courage as moral base-points, you increasingly become lovers of your own humanity and creatureliness, lovers of human and other created beings, and you strive more naturally to practice love, make justice, and advocate for justice-love in all realms of your life together. It gets easier as these moral commitments and capacities become more deeply integrated not only into your personal lives but into your circles of friends and colleagues in the struggles for a more decent and just society.

What you say to me is that this spiritual goal is ours, not just mine; it is a collective project, not simply a personal spiritual agenda—to embody, share, and weave these moral capacities into our common life and projects. This is a primary benefit of belonging to groups of social and political activists and to participating in worshipping congregations that are rooted and grounded in a shared passion for justice, compassion, and peace. Without friends and colleagues who are themselves rooted and grounded in empathy, kindness, compassion, and courage, it's almost impossibly hard to sustain these moral capacities in our lives.

Without you, Christepona, along with my best friends and loved ones here and now on this planet, I don't know whether I myself could, and I don't know that I do very well anyhow. But with your help and by your grace and encouragement, I do what I can. Today.

Hate: A Wasted Emotion

CHRISTEPONA, YOUR ENTHUSIASM FOR these moral capacities reminds me of a story in the news some time ago, when Speaker of the US House of Representatives Nancy Pelosi responded to a journalist's question: "Do you hate the president?"

Pelosi responded that she doesn't hate anyone.

2021 note: Referring to Donald Trump, Pelosi had said she found his policies cowardly and cruel but that, as a lifelong Catholic, she didn't hate the man but rather prayed for him.

Here's what Pelosi was saying: Hate is a wasted emotion. It is rooted in fear, and Speaker Pelosi does not let fear shape her life and work. Her goal is too important.

Hate grows from one root. Yet it can take opposite, but closely related, forms in your life together. The root of all hate is the uneasy moral alliance of your very human fear of danger with your also very human tendency to feel powerless in relation to whatever you fear. Your fear, and your senses of being powerless, are not in themselves moral or spiritual problems. The hatred that your fear and powerless feelings spawn can be very much a moral problem and a spiritual challenge, depending on how you use it.

With fear as a common root, and closely related psychologically, the two forms hate can take among human beings present themselves as stark opposites in your collective life.

One form your hatred can take is toward injustice, oppression, cruelty, and violence. If employed nonviolently, your hatred of evil can be morally constructive and creative, a common human response to injustice and oppression, cruelty and violence against yourselves, other humans, other creatures, or the earth. This hatred is a deep visceral protest against the damages being done by evildoers. The hatred is often felt toward the evildoers themselves: white supremacists, misogynists, homophobes, perpetrators of violence and abuse against more vulnerable creatures, narcissistic blowhards against those with less power.

The second form your hatred can take is the blaming of "others," who you believe have stolen something from you, or from other people, or from the earth and its many creatures. This form of hatred is also common. You recoil against what you experience as theft. You hate those you believe have stolen something from you or from others whom you care about. Not only does this thievery take away something that is rightfully yours, you believe. This thievery is also a dishonest maneuver, an insult to you and your people, a social slap in your face.

For example, those on the political right in America often hate those they imagine are robbing them of their rights to bear arms or to control their own lives and businesses, or who are stripping away their religious or cultural legacies. Those on the left often hate those they believe are stealing bread and justice from the poor, or who are trying to dominate the lives of racial, ethnic, or religious minorities, or who wish to control the lives of women and gendered minorities, or who are robbing the earth of its resources.

The hatred of "others," whom you experience as thieves, regardless of your politics, is not just an American problem. Around the world, and throughout history, people have demonstrated hatred toward those whom they regard as thieves, dishonest rogues, of one kind or another.

Among social and religious conservatives throughout history, hate-filled violence is directed at "outsiders," immigrants, people of minority races, gender identities, and religions. Blame for hard economic times is scapegoated onto "other" races, cultures, nations, genders, and sexual and religions minorities. From social and religious liberals comes hatred and sometimes violence toward leaders of political, economic, and religious organizations and movements perceived to promote injustice. *On the right and left of your politics today, in America and elsewhere, hatred is embodied today in the loathing of your ideological and political opponents.*

In either form—hatred of injustice or hatred of "others"—hatred reflects your fear, whether or not it is warranted. You fear that you or those whom you care about are in danger. You fear that you and others are powerless against those inflicting harm, those who have stolen your rights, your food, whatever you believe you or those you care about need to survive or thrive.

In both forms—hatred against oppression, or hatred against those whom you think are depriving you and those you care about of something you need—hate is a strong visceral reaction against those whom you perceive, accurately or not, to be harming either you or others. In both cases, you hate those whom you experience as a threat to you, your family, your world, your nation, your culture, your people, or to creatures, values, and traditions that you cherish.

This is so true, Christepona, and it's also important for us to keep in mind that hate is not simply an emotion or a feeling. Of course it is a feeling and an attitude, but it's also a gut-call to action. And so we have to be strategic with our hate. We need to think about what we are saying and doing whenever we feel hatred toward others, even those who hate us.

In a strategic moment, Speaker Nancy Pelosi cited the power of prayer—she could just as easily have said love—rather than hatred to eventually bring to justice the powers of evil at work in the world around her. She was lifting up a learned political as well as spiritual practice—the practice of neighbor-love, including enemy-love—as not only a morally righteous attitude but also a more effective political strategy than hatred can ever be.

To show love, or compassion, or to pray for those who wound us or others is not to feel good about them, nor to make a weak or uneasy peace with them. To love our enemies is to refuse to assault with hatred those who are themselves hateful evildoers and, instead, to pray for them. It is also to work day and night to defeat them and prevent the harm they inflict. We must never confuse the refusal to hate people with any acceptance of the evil they do.

In praying for someone we perceive to be an evildoer, we are basically holding open some time and space for them to convert—to turn around and do what is right—perhaps even beyond the bounds of time and space as we know it. We are calling them into *kairos,* some "time beyond time," to turn from evil and do what is good. That is the essence of prayer on behalf of evildoers.

So while we may and often do *feel* hate, rage, and any number of strong negative emotions, against our enemies in this world, our refusal to hate them is to step beyond the realm of personal emotions onto a larger stage in the belief, both spiritually grounded and politically strategic, that love—including a refusal to make peace with evil and oppression—is stronger than hate. And it is so true that love is stronger than the fear that breeds hatred.

Much like Jesus and other prophetic siblings we could name—the recently departed Elijah Cummings and John Lewis come to mind—Speaker Pelosi knows that we humans are not powerless in relation to the forces of evil at work around us. That is probably why she is in politics and why she is a Democrat at this moment in American history, believing in the power of our human capacity for goodness to overcome evil. No doubt, Pelosi has also learned that hate is a wasted emotion. Like clutter, hatred takes up too much mental space to be stored, much less lugged around as baggage.

Moreover, this exceptionally well-seasoned speaker of the House has surely learned that expressions of hate constitute strategic setbacks in the political realm. This woman is too spiritually grounded and politically savvy to sustain hatred for anyone, regardless of her personal feelings, which are really not our business. Pelosi's political aim is to oust a particularly hateful man from the presidency as soon as possible.

2021 note: She did exactly this, with the help of 81,283,098 Americans in November 2020. Joe Biden was elected by 51.3 percent of the popular vote, in a contest hailed by many—from center to the far left of the political spectrum—as probably the most important election in American history. Of course, it will also be remembered for Donald Trump's maniacal refusal to accept the results, which incited the violent insurrection at the US Capitol on January 6, 2021, and subsequent assaults on American democracy.

Faith: Driving the Future

I BELIEVE THAT FAITH holds the key to it all—faith in the power of justice-love making, faith in the power of our struggles for mutuality to carry us through. Some of us affirm our faith in God, Goddess, Mother-Father, higher power, spirit of life, root of moral courage, wellspring of living waters, source of all goodness. Others back away from both the experience of faith and the word "faith" and prefer to rely on, and speak of, humanity's access to what they experience as more reasonable and empirical sources of power for generating goodness.

This book is rooted entirely in my faith. Those of you who've come this far with me at the very least may be finding something of interest here. I realize that perhaps you do, or perhaps you do not, affirm, with me, faith in the power of the One who is speaking to us now, faith in Christepona, she whose names, genders, languages, colors, and shapes are as many and varied as we are, she who reaches toward us on these pages. If you are not, by your own definition, a person of faith, I appreciate your coming along with us on this faith-journey that must seem quite alien to you. Please do not mistake my enthusiasm here for any presumption that you share, or wish to share, or even should share, the root experience—the faith that brings these pages to life.

Carter, we are speaking to you through your faith, not through the experiences of those who do not share it. You are right to honor their different experiences from yours of how you, and they, make meaning of your life together in the world. If there are ways in which your journey in faith touches, or makes sense to others, wonderful. If not, let them be. *They have their ways, their paths, their own frameworks for making meaning.*

On the matter of faith, we are speaking to you in particular, dear Carter, and to other people of faith who can, and do, believe along with you in the mysteries of the spiritual power that infuses our words.

Your faith is the foundation of your staying power and of your best contributions to the common good: Faith, not your religious beliefs, whatever they may be. Faith, not whatever theological doctrines you may espouse. Faith, not necessarily your spiritual practices, though they may nurture your faith. All of these resources—religious credos, theological teachings, spiritual practices—may be tremendously important, sometimes vital, to your lives in community and as individuals. But your personal faith and your collective faith are the deepest, sturdiest, most reliable roots of all.

Faith is your most reliable, future-driven energy. Individually, at a personal level, faith is your heart leaping toward a future being shaped even now by your love, and ours, for one another at all levels of your life together and ours with you. Collectively, your faith is the reaching, stretching, leaning together toward the future on the basis of your experiences of a power you trust to move through you—with us—to create a more justice-loving world. Whether deeply personal or more communitarian, your faith is the casting of your lots with the staying power of truth and goodness—mutuality—to see you through.

Your faith has various origins, depending on who you are. But the strongest most persistent faith always has roots in your personal and communal experiences of the transformative power of justice-love, or the power of mutual relation, in the smaller and larger arenas of your life together.

Your scripture, those of you who are Christian, offers a wonderful image for faith: Like the tiniest mustard seed, your faith grows into the most magnificent tree that provides nourishment, shade, beauty, and a resting place for all who are struggling for a more just, humane, creation-affirming world.[1]

1. See Matt 13:30–32; Mark 4:30–32; Luke 13:19.

Intuition and Reason

MANY OF US CAN affirm the power of faith. But how, Christepona, do we know anything for sure? In shaping these words, yours and mine, how do you or we know what we are talking about? How do we speak with confidence in temporal realms of either *chronos* or *kairos*, or of good and evil?

This is an important question because so many do not realize that knowledge—knowing anything—is grounded in intuition. Intuitive knowledge is often preconscious, elusive, elastic, less able to be boxed in cognitively, less able to be controlled. Your intuition alerts you to an encroaching storm, and your reason tells you to fill the water jugs in case you lose electricity. You don't choose between intuition and reason; they function together.

We who are Christepona came to Carter first through intuition and imagination and, because she responded with an open mind and yearning heart, we are privileged to meet others of you in realms where reason and intuition coexist and sometimes mutually reinforce and strengthen each other.

How do we know? How do you know? The power of human reason—to think things through, to study and analyze and reflect on data and information—has been a bedrock of human history, but not without intuition. Many fail to see that reason and intuition, including imagination, go hand in hand in shaping human knowledge and history.

Intuition is a spontaneous way of knowing what springs up through your hearts and souls and infuses your capacity to reason. Intuition is most often experienced through your feelings. Whether in love or worship; art or music; poetry, prayer, or meditation, intuitive knowledge rises up within you, seeking a voice or a form of expression. Intuition is inspirational knowledge and is the motivating energy of creativity as well as spiritual energy. The lives and contributions of such artists as Americans Georgia O'Keefe (1887–1986), Toni Morrison (1931–2019), Lin-Manuel Miranda (b. 1980), and Chilean Isabel Allende (b. 1942) are infused by intuition. But these artists have also been powered by reason. Intuition need not be, and is usually not, unreasonable because, truthfully, in the lives and work of people who are not only reasonable but wise, intuition is as much a source of knowledge as any books or lessons on scientific method.

Reason presents itself as a more linear cognitive process and is experienced as the process of thinking. Reason tells you one plus one equals two, seeds need water, horses eat grass, cars burn fuel. Via your brains' cognitive powers, you work toward knowing whatever you must in order to make sense of your lives, relationships, work, world, and the countless problems you encounter. The knowledge you acquire through reason can be powerful, creative, constructive, mind-boggling, and infinitely fascinating.

If artists represent the power of intuition, scientists are the masters of reason. The lives and work of German physicist Albert Einstein (1879–1955) and the various Nobel Laureates in economics and the so-called natural sciences and mathematics exemplify the power of reason. But reason has little creative energy unless it is guided, and strengthened, by intuition.

The lives and work of scientists like German physician and humanitarian Albert Schweitzer (1875–1965) and English anthropologist/primatologist Jane Goodall (b. 1934) demonstrate that intuition has played significant parts in their knowing what to do next and in discerning the probable value of taking one path and not another in their research. Schweitzer and Goodall's relationships with the world around them and with animals have been shaped by both their own intuitive powers and their experiences of animals' capacities to intuit and to reason. Understanding animals and creation as co-subjects rather than simply as objects of human research, many humans have realized—intuited and reasoned—animals' esteemed place among humans as not only sentient beings but also as creatures whose intuition and reason tell them where to live, whom to trust, and how to plan the future.

Similarly, in relation to the created world of shifting tectonic plates, trees, rivers, and mountains, scientists like Danish seismologist Inge Lehmann (1888–1993) and American geographer and geologist Mary Arizona "Zonia" Baber (1862–1956) seemed to have sensed from childhood—where intuitive power is often born and is strongest—that creation is infused with knowledge that eludes all but the most attentive humans and that many compelling scientific breakthroughs have sturdy roots in subjective human experience as well as in the more objective realms of academic research.

Our point is that, among animals and humans, intuition and reason work together. Without either, knowledge is untrustworthy and truth is suspect. You, Carter, and countless others, have learned—intuitively you may have always known—that your cognitive gifts are strengthened by your intuitive powers and, vice-versa, that your intuition is sharpened through your capacities to reason. This has been true throughout human history. Knowledge has a yin/yang shape, forged by an interplay of intuition and reason—whenever people and creatures of any species are closest to the truth. That is as true here in these pages as it is in other resources of spirituality, ethics, social studies, earth science, or political discourse.

Isn't all human knowledge rooted and grounded in experience, and isn't our experience, basically, the intuitive soil in which knowledge—even the most abstract or empirical knowledge—can grow? Can any truth, ever, be entirely separate from some degree of intuition and imagination? Isn't this why Mongolian shamans, for example, view horses as sources of sacred wisdom and remarkable intuition that gives rise to practical knowledge, such as how to find people who are lost in the desert and where to find food or water when there seems to be none anywhere around? Shamans, sages, and other wise women and men teach us that knowledge is simply what we know, and that much of what we know cannot be measured or recorded.[1]

---

1. Isaacson, *Horse Boy*.

Capitalist Spirituality

THE GREAT CHRISTIAN FEMINIST social ethicist Beverly Wildung Harrison—now on the other side and a chief participant in Christepona—was one of my life partners for over three decades and a beloved friend for half a century. She was also the most brilliant academic I've ever known, regarded widely by students and colleagues as better able than anyone to build a persuasive argument in ethics and moral theology, drawing from social theory and science as well as the daily news, in making her case. At the same time, no scholar made a better case for the power of intuition, imagination, and feeling in building sound scholarly presentations.

One of her intellectual and intuitive passions until the day she died was in making connections between the political economy (advanced global capitalism) and what she called "capitalist spirituality." Beverly Harrison understood, intellectually, that dominant economic and religious systems are always interactive—and she also knew in her bones and gut, through her life as a Christian in an advanced capitalist society, that something was wrong, badly wrong, with how our economic system is structured.

With Beverly Harrison as one of the strongest voices in Christepona, she and I will lay out the framework here for how she understood capitalist spirituality, as I heard her then and continue to hear her now, in this critical moment in which christofascism and COVID-19 are on the rise together.

I am framing this section of the book in my voice rather than Christepona's to share some of what Bev and I talked about in months leading up to her death in 2012 and also what I continue to "hear" through her spiritual prodding. This ongoing conversation about capitalist spirituality with Bev predates Christepona's entrance into my life, though I have no doubt that Beverly Harrison's strong views on the state of capitalist spirituality are infusing Christepona's perspective and urgency.

The great social problems and spiritual challenges that face us now are steeped in our collective failure, as Americans in particular, to grasp the extent to which we are not, and should not aspire to be, basically on our own, independent of all others, able to fend for ourselves. We often feel like we are just that—individual pieces being moved around, like on a giant board game of Monopoly, being played by the wealthiest (mostly white men) on the planet. Given the basically individualistic messages we receive from both capitalism and Christianity, we learn—especially those of us with Protestant Christian roots—that our individual selves are our basic social, economic, psychological, and spiritual units.

But no. To the contrary, we are never simply on our own from spiritual, psychological, social, or economic perspectives. Our lives are systemically, constantly, and forever bound together in our living and dying. We are never alone. Each of us is involved with all of us. Our "we-ness" shapes my "I-ness."[1] The Hebrew prophets as well as the Christian Gospel writers knew this. We are connected in our social, moral, and spiritual accomplishments as well as our problems. We are connected through our capacities and our incapacities to contribute to the whole of who we are as societies and communities. Our oneness is shaped out of our many varied talents and treasures, as well as out of our failures and disappointments.

The morally mistaken notion that each of us should or can make it on our own, or else fall by the wayside, has been cultivated through the merger of the most morally mistaken and socially destructive edges of capitalism as an economic system and Christianity as a religion. We see evidence of this deadly convergence today

---

1. In 1987, psychologist Janet L. Surrey, an Associate at Wellesley College's Stone Center, and I met and became devoted friends and colleagues in a shared, interdisciplinary study of the mutuality we both perceive as the heart of all healthy, life-giving, and sacred relationships. Our exploration of the many dimensions of this truth continues to this day.

in the insistence of most conservative Republican and Christian political, economic, and religious leaders that each of us is on her or his own to beat back the coronavirus any way we can, each of us, and each of our families, and each of our states. We are on our own not only with respect to the COVID virus but in relation to the whole of our lives—as individuals who love and work, sink or swim, live and die, on our own, and that's how we "keep America great." Notice the ongoing co-optation by political leaders of many evangelical Protestant Christians, who have attached their faith to an economic agenda which largely serves to increase the wealth of the super-rich.[2] This is "capitalist spirituality" in action.

2021 note: This situation grew increasingly grim under the Trump administration's abdication of corporate responsibility for the health of the people, a failure magnified by Trump's co-optation of large segments of evangelical Protestant Christianity, as both political and spiritual leaders preached a "my way or the highway" form of dedicated individualism.

Here is how Beverly Harrison understood this ungodly merger of capitalism and Christianity:

Against the late feudal, rigidly hierarchical arrangement of economic power in eighteenth century Europe, "capitalism" emerged as a promising alternative. Scotsman Adam Smith (1723–1790) envisioned a chicken in the pot of every family, an early capitalist icon of possibility. What if every man (white men only of course) was encouraged socially and legally to earn money (capital) for his own work and, thereby, could actually provide for his own family? Could this not become a more just and humane economic social foundation than the feudal control of economic resources by lords born to the manor? Harrison believed that early capitalism offered a just and creative vision for a particular time and place in history.

In her project, she would have attempted to correlate the evolution of capitalism as an economic system developing alongside

---

2. Du Mez, *Jesus and John Wayne*.

Christianity during the same period.[3] In what she tagged conversationally as "capitalist spirituality," Harrison would have made connections between advanced global capitalism's growing obsession with ever-increasing profit for the world's wealthiest few—the 1 percent—and Protestant Christianity's raising up of the salvation of the individual's soul as *more basic* to Christian mission than our collective well-being and shared social responsibility for one another's safety, health, and happiness.

Harrison contended that capitalist spirituality in the modern and postmodern West is rooted in the assumption that each person is on his or her own in relation to a God who connects with us primarily as individuals on private spiritual journeys. Through capitalist spirituality, all humans are entitled by God to *possess* (a capitalist notion) what we believe to be our God-given rights to personal freedom *over* collective responsibilities to care for one another. Our spiritual and moral assumptions as capitalists emphasize our personal rights, freedom, and privileges *over* our social responsibilities as citizens to care for our nations, for all people, and for our planet home. This is especially the case in the Christian West in which, Harrison maintained, capitalist spirituality is the prevailing civil religion in the twenty-first century.

Harrison would have stressed the devolution over several centuries of both capitalism and Protestant Christianity from their origins as *protest movements—reformations—for justice* against the oppressive practices of feudalism and, earlier, the Roman Catholic church's demand for obedience to ecclesiastical authority, indulgences, and other practices of paying homage—and money of course—to the church, in exchange for salvation.

Given the reliable shape of her life and work as a prophetic Christian teacher, Beverly Harrison, we can be sure, would have presented her work on capitalist spirituality as a wake-up call for her siblings to continue the reformations of both capitalism and Christianity and, for that matter, of other religious traditions around the world whose neighbor-loving origins have been obscured by the relentless greed of advanced global capitalism.

3. Harrison, *Justice in the Making*, 153–219.

Ever making connections, Beverly Harrison would have attempted to show the extent to which advanced global capitalism, without significant pushback from mainstream Christianity in the West, has served largely the economic interests of wealthy white men and those over whom they claim "rights" of ownership or entitlement: "their" women, children, slaves, servants, or other subordinate peoples and creatures, including the earth itself.

More than anything, Beverly Harrison would have urged her sisters and brothers to push back, resist, and revolt against the unholy alliance of economic greed and spiritual narcissism, especially in contemporary American society where a morally repugnant capitalist spirituality stirs the base of a christofascist president and his nativist, white supremacist, and misogynist economic agenda.

2021 note: Beverly Harrison would have been thrilled, and relieved, by Biden's victory in 2020, but she would have participated in her ongoing work as a fierce critic of capitalist spirituality. I am confident she would be pushing Joe Biden's administration toward greater economic oversight and regulation as well as critiquing the church's reticence to become an outspoken adversary of capitalist spirituality. I may be projecting here, but I think I'm not when I say that Bev would have been increasingly an outspoken proponent of democratic socialism and might well have linked up with Elizabeth Warren's campaign and ongoing projects.

Turning to Jesus

As participants in Christepona, Beverly Harrison and Dorothee Soelle push us to think about "capitalist spirituality" and "christofascism" and how they are connected. And now they turn to me with an interesting question:

We ask you, Carter, in the context of the capitalist spirituality that thrives today in christofascist America and other parts of the predominantly Christian world—Protestant, Catholic, Orthodox— why does Jesus matter so much to you and other liberal Christians? We know, of course, what your answer is, but we believe it's important for you to share this with those who are reading this book: Why, for G-d's sake, does what the churches, even the liberal churches, teach about Jesus matter in the slightest to people who are neither Christian, white, male, nor wealthy?

Fair enough. Let me tell you what I think, dear readers. What Christians believe about Jesus matters not only to our faith but moreover to how we treat ourselves, one another, all other humans and cultures and religions, all creatures great and small, and the earth. In that sense, what we Christians believe or don't believe about Jesus matters to other people, regardless of their religion, and to creatures and to the earth itself. This is because we Christians, like people of all religious traditions on the planet— especially those with significant amounts of economic and other forms of political power—can do great harm to our earth. Or we can choose to heal its people and creatures.

But, Christepona persists, *why does a dead man from Nazareth and, for many, his resurrected spirit, matter to Christians— whether orthodox or radical, conservative or liberal, whatever their* national, cultural, racial-ethnic, gendered, or political identities? Why Jesus in particular?

Let's not only ask Carter. Let's ask Jesus, who's here with us in Christepona. Let him speak for himself.

And so here I imagine Jesus speaking, his voice shaped and spoken in contemporary American English and structured much as I, Carter, would hear Jesus chatting with me, as a friend or elder brother, a spiritual teacher or fellow activist, walking in the woods with my dogs and me. This may strike you as wildly audacious or as bogus. But let me ask you, some of you at least, what do *you* mean when you imagine yourself listening to Jesus or any of the saints or to God/Goddess in prayer?

Jesus begins speaking:

Be clear at the outset that I'm not speaking as, nor about, myself symbolically as the mythic figurehead of one of the world's major religions. Don't get hung up on all my fancy titles. After all, I don't know myself as any king, prince, lord, or savior. I'm here with you, Carter. I'm here in the spiritual community of Christepona. You know me already. I am Jesus, a real human being, who was born, lived, and died two millenia ago in a part of the world most Americans refer to as the Middle East. Palestine was my home. Judaism was my religion. The Roman Empire was our colonizer and overlord, the power that set the terms for who lived and who died, people just like me.

If my story as a human being matters to people, as it does to many people on the earth, it's because they find something compelling in the story of how I lived and died, something that helps them set their moral compasses by which they try to live meaningful lives. Christians assume that I had a special relationship to G-d, and they want one too, just like you do, Carter.

Still, you Christians actually know very little about me. Here's what most of you think you know:

I was born to Mary, a young Jewish woman who lived in the heart of the land which today is part of Palestine's West Bank. Christians believe I was raised by Mary and Joseph, a carpenter who had accompanied Mary during her pregnancy and had been present at my birth. According to your Bible, Mary and Joseph had traveled from their hometown, Nazareth, to pay taxes in the city of Bethlehem. It is said that, after I was born in Bethlehem, Mary and Joseph fled with me out of the country. Christians have believed that our family followed a star toward Egypt in order to escape Herod the Great's order that all baby boys be slaughtered. According to tradition, King Herod had wished to make sure no male child would live to displace him as King of the Jews, a prophecy which had distressed him. So Joseph and Mary took flight with their baby boy. It's a good story about a refugee family.

Most scholars of the period do not believe that this "slaughter of the innocents" actually occurred. As a boy, I never heard a word about it. But whether or not historically true, the story sets the stage both for more liberal Christianity's portrayal of my family as a poor refugee family—refugee or not, like most Palestinians, we were poor—and for more conservative Christianity's core teaching that my meaning and my value were largely symbolic: I was the Christ, Messiah, Savior, myself a king, though not over the temporal order as Herod had feared.

Beyond the Christian Bible, there is only passing mention of me in other historical accounts of the period. For most of my life, I was a preacher and teacher in Galilee, which is located in the northeastern part of today's Israel, across the Sea of Galilee from the Golan Heights, most recently part of the country you know as Syria. In 1967, the Golan Heights was annexed by Israel.

I spent several years preaching and teaching about the presence of G-d—the source and spirit of Love with and among all humans and creatures on earth. This is really all the early evangelists knew and reported about me, and it's all that really matters anyhow. They also knew that I was crucified—executed—by the Roman Empire because the king and other Roman leaders feared my popularity might launch an insurrection against the government.

But here's the strange part and, from my perspective, a pity. Over the centuries, from the earliest days of the church, people who have identified as my followers—Christians—have held serious, often deadly, deliberations to determine who's in and who's out, who's right and who's wrong about my relationship to G-d both before and after my death. Those who've been deemed wrong by the political and religious powers that be have been crucified, banished, burned, beheaded, or otherwise disposed of by state and church leaders. The leaders of states and churches have persecuted people less because of any real interest in my story or in connecting spiritually with me than because they feared that the others—the "losers"—were threats to their power, enemies to the power structures of the state or church or often both. Perhaps they were. But I have always regarded it as a sorrow and a pity that so many—mostly innocent people doing what they believed was right and often willing to live peaceably and nonviolently with their opponents—have been killed in my name. This is not what I lived or died for and to this day it breaks my heart.

Let's be honest. My name has been used less as a symbol of love and justice in ecclesiastical trials and debates than as a political pawn of power-brokers struggling for control over the lives, allegiances, and financial resources of my followers.

Beginning shortly after my death and extending several hundred years into the growth of the early church, many Christians came to believe that I was uniquely the Christ, the Son of G-d, the Lord and Savior of humankind, whose presence had been foretold by the prophets of Israel. Moreover, these churchmen (for the most part, males) proposed that I be understood as "fully divine and fully human"—that is, that I be understood as divine, G-d himself in human form. Me and only me, a divine man.

At the same time, from the beginning, some of my followers— usually a minority, once the church became aligned with the Roman Empire under the Emperor Constantine—have questioned putting me on such a lofty doctrinal pedestal as a uniquely divine man, and as Lord and Christ of all. These Christians, often condemned by the powers of church and state as heretics, have often insisted that I was a fully human brother whose life and story became a window into how G-d acts in history—through people loving one another and the G-d Spirit that connects them—up until the present time.

This latter image—of me as a fully human brother—describes how you understand me, Carter, and I too believe that's pretty much who I was and am. But all humans embody multiple meanings and we all have layers of understanding who we, and others, are, do we not? You and your friends and colleagues, like me. We are all perceived differently by various people for their own particular reasons. My being designated "Christ" for and by many Christians is not a pity in and of itself. It's a pity and a shame only because Christians so often use this title they gave me—"Christ"—to wield power over those who are not Christians as well as over their own Christian siblings, those whose beliefs about me are quite different from their own. This wielding of power-over invariably leads to violence and evil. I will say it again— it's a great pity and a profound sorrow, an everlasting sorrow, that my story continues to be exploited in this way.

But you, Carter, and others who experience me as a human brother must surely realize that you too can become arrogant in imagining that your way is the right way, even the only way, to understand who I was and am. I celebrate your way of seeing and knowing me, because it is how I most clearly understood and understand myself.

But how can I be so smug as to imagine that I, and only I, can understand the meanings of my own life and death? And how can you? I cannot make this mistake, and you must not make it either. We must always err on the side of humility. Because we do not know it all, even about ourselves, our own lives and meanings, much less the lives and meanings and symbolic power accorded to those who've gone before us.

As long as religious leaders, including you and other liberals as well as all the conservatives, insist that there is only one right creed or one right set of beliefs, including beliefs about me, and only one way to worship G-d, there will be religious conflict and violence. This was true two millennia ago, and it is true today.

If people lift me up as the one and only way to G-d, they inevitably set themselves up as the true believers, the only ones who are right about G-d and the world. Regardless of their personal intentions, which for many Christians are innocent enough, such true believers are often experienced as lording their one and only right religion over all others. Such religious imperialism, as it is experienced by non-Christians and less "right-thinking" Christians around the world, leads to violence.

I say this again, and again, because it causes me such grief. Wars and conflicts are then waged in my name, which reflects a dreadful, sorrowful, horribly mistaken understanding of my life, who I was, and who I am.

Listen to me, Carter and the rest of you: I lived close to G-d, as close as my next breath. This meant loving at the core of my being and showing my friends how to god, how to love, thereby helping heal and liberate the spirits and bodies of my sisters and brothers, simply that, no more, no less.

But let me say this before I turn this back over to my sisters and brothers in Spirit: Whenever and wherever you lift me up as your Lord and Savior—which is what most Christians in this world do—may the story of my life, my death, and my ongoing risen Spirit liberate you from hatred, violence, fear, and despair. May you use my name and the symbols you ascribe to me always and only in the service of One whose essence is compassion, forgiveness, hope, and the love that generates justice.

That's the heart and soul of how I understood and understand the meaning of my own life, and yours, you who are writing and reading this book: Love G-d and love one another, enemies and friends alike, the earth and all life no less than human life. Love. Justice-love. In the names of G-d.

May it be so, and thank you for giving me this time and space to speak.

Jesus falls quiet.

Christepona is silent, and so am I.

But after a moment, I ask myself and you, again—what did I *think* it meant, to walk and talk with Jesus, as the old song goes?

A Universal Spirit of Mutual Respect
—Simply Utopic?

BELIEVERS IN JESUS OF *course have no monopoly on spiritual arrogance and religious imperialism except in one important sense: Because dominant religions are bound up with dominant political economies, as Beverly Harrison insists, Christianity in its mainstream has become a global cathedral of capitalist spirituality. Wherever on earth capitalism's tentacles reach and wherever Christianity is a dominant social and economic force, Christian imperialism remains a psycho-spiritual, social and political, root of discrimination and violence toward all wrong-thinking Christians as well toward those who are not Christian.*

Yes, and I would say that, whatever we may believe about our dear brother Jesus, however diverse our views, a key question for Christians in today's christofascist contexts is how to live, practice, and present our spiritualities in a world in which people of different religions and spiritual traditions, including radically disparate views within Christianity itself, urgently need to live together as siblings in a sacred Spirit of mutual respect.

So many traditional Christians, in America and around the world, hate and fear those of us who are queer or feminist or womanist or simply liberal in today's badly divided social orders. And to be honest, we who are liberal or on the radically left margins of the churches fear our more traditional conservative evangelical Protestant, Catholic, and Orthodox Christian siblings. We especially fear their collusion with the powers of the state to make policies that oppress us and others by denying us human rights to love whom we love, marry whom we love, express our genders without fear of being killed, and if we are black or brown, those who deny us the right to walk down the street without being killed by police or others who fear our darkness in white supremacist societies.

This is something neither Christians nor others have done well over time, no doubt because building communities of mutual respect is daunting spiritual and moral work. Still, it is a profoundly worthwhile human goal—to live in, and work toward, peace with our human siblings of various and very different religious, spiritual, and moral traditions.

But honestly, Jesus and others of you in Christepona, we here on earth right now as living humans must ask how there can ever be peaceful coexistence among people of significantly divergent and often discordant religions, spiritualities, and moral traditions?

As well you should ask this question, Carter—and we have a response:

The basis for mutually respectful coexistence of different religions, spiritualities, and moral traditions would be shared affirmations of universal sources, or standards, of goodness and truth. We see of course that such a radical affirmation is utopic—"nowhere yet"—on planet earth.

But let us dream for a moment with you: Such affirmations would be woven out of several brilliant, sturdy fibers:

Acknowledgment of significant differences among yourselves, not only—but primarily—in relation to your spiritual traditions; and yet, at the same time:

Trust in the power of human goodness—your own and that of others—meaning that you trust one another's natural human longings to be loved and respected, and to love and respect others.

Humility in relation to one another—meaning, no one knows it all, ever, about anything, including the Sacred; and that such humility is practiced as a moral foundation of all traditions.

Finally, commitment to nonviolence in your ongoing negotiations for space, time, resources, and voice.

Ah, dream on, you say! Such utopic spinning and sparking on the parts of angels. But bear with us . . .

A UNIVERSAL SPIRIT OF MUTUAL RESPECT—SIMPLY UTOPIC?

You would need to foster mutuality with one another across your different religious and spiritual cultures, building mutuality with roots in respect for your common human rights as siblings to be safe from harm, including your rights to worship or not as you wish, without harming others and without being harmed yourselves.

You would need to trust in the power and presence of a universal source of goodness by whatever names you might call it (or by no names at all) as the most powerful moral force in the universe, stronger than your own evildoing and that of others, and most certainly stronger than any of your intellectual capacities to fully understand who or what this source of goodness is or by what names or images it or she or he or they might best be known.

And while your efforts to be good people—empathic, kind, compassionate, courageous—would contribute to your well-being as people and as a planet, any efforts to be best, or better than others, would be not only unnecessary, but unhelpful and often destructive. In the realm of religious differences, you would see that all desires to be best—smartest, most right, most faithful, most nearly perfect, closest to G-d by whatever names—are not only foolish and futile but moreover are dangerous, and quickly become deadly, aspirations. You would realize that such pompous aspirations are completely counterproductive to living a good life; and, if you are religious, a faithful one.

Humility with respect to your own traditions would be essential. Humility is rooted in the realization that you stand on common ground and share the earth with all humans and creatures and that, in order to be good, or do good, you don't need to be best, nor does anyone else. You need only love one another, which is to demonstrate mutual respect through empathic acts of kindness, compassion, and courage.

A commitment to practice nonviolence would be essential in your efforts to find common ground and respect one another's ways of being who they are, including their religious practices, ways which you may not understand nor probably wish to share, because they would not be yours, and because they would seem strange and alien to your cultural sensibilities. And that would be okay. You would not have to join in religious or spiritual rituals or practices that you chose not to join in.

There would be no place in your world of universal peace and coexistence for the use of bombs or guns, knives or poison, fire or water, stones or sticks, bullying or shunning, lies or humiliations, to destroy or diminish one another, however much you might disapprove of others' spiritual or nonspiritual practices.

Whenever you might strongly disapprove of another's religious tradition—and, of course, most humans have this experience, probably more often than you may wish to admit—your moral challenge would be simply to let others be who they are, do what they do, and worship or not whomever or whatever they please.

But there is a caveat: A nonnegotiable moral condition for all religious traditions and organizations in a world of peaceful religious coexistence would be that your spiritual practices, and those of others, do not harm others.

Now what do we mean by "harm," which is such a slippery and subjective concept? Obviously, we mean violence, violating others—hurting, wounding, torturing, battering, killing them, physically of course, but also mentally, emotionally, spiritually, individually and collectively. Most of you would agree even now that you are morally obligated to try your best not to harm other humans, those close to you, those far away, those whom you know and love, those whom you know and do not like, those whom you do not know at all. "Do no harm" is a maxim of medical ethics and of all reputable professional standards.

Not all of you, nor most humans, will agree that doing no harm applies also to human treatment of animals and earth. But that is another topic, and a huge and major one it is, and we will return to it. Let us just say here that, in a world of peaceful religious coexistence, you would have to do everything in your power to prevent harm being done to humans, yourself and others—and, depending on your own faith tradition or simply your own conscience—to animals and to the earth.

In cases in which harm is being inflicted in accordance with a sacred teaching, you are obligated to stop it if you can, whether or not it is a sacred teaching of your own tradition. Whatever their religious or spiritual roots, if sacred teachings demand harming other people—so-called "honor killings" are one evil example of this—you must do whatever you can to prevent those who do such violence from inflicting it on others without also doing violence to them if at all possible.

That people often fall back on a badly mistaken notion of religious freedom to justify harming others is never, in any case, or in the name of any god, a valid spiritual or moral excuse. It is intolerable to those who are committed to mutually respectful, peaceful religious coexistence.

But really, how can you stop such violence—which, for many of you (and all of us in Christepona) includes all social injustice and discrimination—without doing harm to the perpetrators?

Through communal and personal prayer; through forging humane and just laws; through generating social policies that protect all people from harmful religious practices, social discrimination, and injustice; and through political work on behalf of leaders who are committed to shaping and enforcing such laws and policies.

In such ways, you can work productively toward building a world in which there is more physical, social, psychological, and religious space for all humans, not just some.

Sadly, we who are Christepona know this bar may be impossibly high for most humans right now. Most of you cannot even imagine building foundations for peaceful coexistence among the religions, spiritualities, and moral traditions of the world. But let us say, boldly and truthfully, that from the earliest days of the church, countless visionary spiritual, moral, and political leaders have voiced such dreams generation upon generation. We who are Christepona are among them, and most of us were when we were alive on earth.

We invite you to join us in this irrepressible spirit of hope and courage.

All of you, if you wish, can play parts in shaping spiritualities of universal goodness and in setting down universal moral moorings. You can participate in the more universalist traditions that have taken root and are rising among people in the West and throughout the world. You can help your own religious and spiritual communities—your churches, synagogues, mosques, covens, and other organizations—become more genuinely universalist in their worship, teachings, celebrations, and practices.

We who are Christepona have found ourselves increasingly walking the path of universalism with all who are seeking to walk this path. We urge you to believe us and join us. Our sibling Jesus, here in Christepona, walks this path alongside other saints, prophets, spiritual teachers, moral leaders, and common people and creatures of all kinds, a path that wraps around the earth many times. Our numbers, languages, colors, cultures, and spiritual paths are legion.

Our dream of a common universal peaceful coexistence of moral and spiritual traditions likely will be accomplished only partially, and only dimly. But to the extent that you who are writing and reading this book are willing to help make such universalist spaces more real and vibrant, even in small ways, you are making a gift to the whole creation on behalf of us all, those who have passed and those still present and active on earth.

Tears

NOT TO DWELL ON it, but our tears, ours as well as yours, are not irrelevant to what we are saying and hearing. From far beyond the grave they well up, our tears, and they come. Oh, do they come, slowly forming a drop at a time or pouring over us and through us, we who live in memory or flesh. Our tears are washing us, and you, in pain, sadness, sorrow, horror, rushing over your cheeks and bones and through the energizing spirit of our presence. They come and they come, in sadness or fear, coursing through us like personal and transpersonal waterfalls of meaning, memory, confusion, exhaustion, and senses of despair.

But then too, how often our tears are bathing us and you in pools of empathy, kindness, compassion, and courage as they surge up from the wellsprings of our common humankind, creature-kind, and shared divinity, because they most surely do, our tears welling up and pouring down, often steeped in sorrow but also in joy for whatever we most cherish, even as we move on beyond.

Our tears spring from that place—soul—where we meet you in a power that is sacred because it is shared. Our tears well up in us to wash away any notion that we, Christepona, or you, our author and readers, are simply on our own, any of us, ever, in kairos. Our tears signal we are siblings moving together through pain, fear, terror, sorrow. Our tears carry us down streams of loss and grief, streams of sadness too deep for words, currents of confusion, relief, despair, and sometimes intimations of hope, and so on and so on. Our tears bear us along in common creaturely experiences, often unimaginably heartbreaking, and almost always reflections of having loved or been loved in our daily lives or at least in our dreams.

TEARS OF CHRISTEPONA

Our tears—sometimes flowing from inspiration and joy—tell us the truth and empower us to touch our common humanity and creature-kind. For this reason, tears can motivate us to feel and act more decisively on behalf of our common well-being. But because tears wash away our pretenses and reveal our true selves, tears—our own and those of others—can also frighten us and tamp down our capacities for empathy and compassion, kindness and connection.

Yes. Tears, tears, and more tears...

I lost Feather on April 21, 2020, almost six months after her diagnosis. Her death was as sorrowful as any moment in my life has ever been or could ever be. Not that others—human loved ones and other creatures—have not mattered to me as much. Not that I have not loved others as much. In truth, I have loved each cherished companion "most" or "best" in her or his own way—always in relation to who the beloved has been in her/his own special self, and always in relation to who the loved one has been to me, and always in relation to the particular time and space in which we have loved, and lost, each other. Death gets easier the older we get only in the sense that it is more familiar and we are no longer shocked by such sorrow.

Like Red, her mom, Feather came into my life just when I needed her equine energy and presence most, to accompany me as I become an older woman in the world, seeking meaning and purpose, wanting to live more deeply in the Spirit of Justice-Love and Joy and Gratitude.

Like Red, but in some ways even more so, because Feather was a youngster as I was becoming more aware of my own aging processes, Feather mentored me with a young energy and fresh openness to each new day.

Like Red before her, Feather became my chief spirit guide, my most reliable source of a shamanic Wisdom that often comes through horses because:

they listen deeply
they live fully in the present
they are loyal to their herd and their humans
they are gentle herbivores

they are simultaneously magnificent in their power
yet ever-so-vulnerable to injury and disease
they are God-bearers, Spirit-filled incarnations
truly priests to those who turn to them
as I turned to Red and her daughter
Feather.

I laid sobbing, my head on Feather's body lying on the ground, having fallen almost as gently as a feather. My friend and Feather's doctor, Kris, laid sobbing with me, both of us on Feather's body, tears pouring over each other, onto Feather, and into the ground.

Tears tell us the truth and empower us to touch our shared humanity, creatureliness, divinity, and share sorrows too deep for words, and so they did.

Aftermath

IN THE WAKE OF *Feather's death, we Christepona had few words, but much strong presence.*

We surrounded Carter and Sue and Kris and Sandi and Josh and Jody and Nancy and Jenn and Preston and dogs Bailey and Joy and horses Breaker and Sophie and Joe and kitties Velvet and Barry, all those who had gathered in that sorrowful moment with Feather and Carter. We were there, holding them up, whether or not they saw us or knew that we were there. We did our best to assure them of our presence and power working through their love and loss and sadness and friendships. We trusted that our presence would comfort them going forward.

It's just as well that Carter had almost completed writing this manuscript with us at the time of Feather's death, because all she could do in the aftermath of this great sorrow was walk and sleep and cry and sleep and walk some more with her dogs and be mindful especially of the other horses in their grief at the loss of their pasture mate.

Forgiveness

Wrapping ourselves tenderly around Carter's heart in the wake of Feather's death, we Christepona are ourselves filled with empathy, yet we also are trembling with anger at the christofascist—transparently racist, economically exploitative, greedy, profit-driven—responses in America to the COVID-19 pandemic that surrounds us all.

This pervasive evil disrupts even the sacred sorrow shared by Carter and her companions in the moment of Feather's death. So holding them close—Carter, Kris, Sue and the others—comforting them, we also turn to another task. This shows you how it works in kairos: *Our spiritual energies spin and spark and move in many directions at once and yet we are never depleted because we share the load, and we rest and refresh as we must.*

Noting our loathing of those who care more about themselves than about the suffering of the world, we realize we must speak here of forgiveness because, in our raging against evil, we know well that without forgiveness, humanity is lost. You are lost, and so are we.

So let us speak to you about forgiveness.

The only way to forgive those in the crosshairs of your anger, and ours, is to detach ourselves from them—not spiritually, but emotionally, which is more of a problem for you who live on earth than for those of us who've moved on further into kairos. *We are not as emotionally driven as you are, which is not to say we do not remember how it was for us once upon a time in* chronos. *We know well how it is for you. We reach out for you in your emotional turmoil to help you—here and now—forgive others much as you seek to be forgiven yourselves.*

In order to forgive, always in a spirit of oneness with us, you need a glimpse of yourselves, us, and others, past and present, including your enemies, sharing space and time in a world that seems hopelessly shattered.

The more honestly you can imagine our oneness with you as humanity and creature-kind, if only fleetingly, the more clearly you will see yourselves together when you are mutually related—and also realize sadly, often tragically, when you are not.

In fear and hatred, ignorance or apathy, many people shut you out—not primarily because they do not know you but because they do not know themselves, and they are afraid to get to know either themselves or you. The better you can detach yourselves emotionally from them, the more likely you can forgive them.

In spirit and in truth, such people deserve your pity more than your loathing. We are speaking here of people who enrage not only you, but us as well: people who rip children from their parents, defend white supremacy, advocate ever-increasing wealth for the wealthiest among you regardless of the economic toll this imbalance takes on the poorest among you; people who care not a whit for the unborn once they are born and who have little or no empathy or sympathy for women and girls who are forced to be pregnant; people at best indifferent to the health of our planet and too often contemptuous of those who live in solidarity with an endangered earth; people whose fear has led them to distrust and even hate those whose colors, cultures, genders, religions, ideologies, or species are unlike their own. These are pathetic, broken people.

You can detach emotionally from these dreadfully mistaken siblings more easily if you see that you too have participated in the production of, and often enjoy, the very evils they embrace, whether or not you personally have meant to do so.

You can detach emotionally from those whom you loathe only if you realize that, often in ranting against their wickedness, you are failing to realize ways in which you or your ancestors are implicated along with them in the doing of evil.

FORGIVENESS

Jesus voiced a prayer: "Forgive us our sins as we forgive those who sin against us."[1] *He also asked G-d to forgive those who "don't know what they're doing."*[2] *Hang on to these lessons, because they are among Jesus' and our, Christepona's, greatest wisdom teachings to offer you and all humankind.*

If you really experience yourselves rooted and grounded in these spiritual lessons, you can forgive one another—and yourselves—and experience a little more peace of mind.

But remember that forgiveness is not a free pass, not now, not ever. Do not forget the evil being done, and do not condone or pacify those who are doing it.

You do not need to like, much less befriend, those whose behavior you despise or—at a very personal level—those who have hurt you. You need not keep these people as friends on a personal level—although occasionally you and they may surprise one another. If they have hurt you and then have turned away from possibilities of forgiveness, pray for them and release them into the kairos, *where we will look after them, believe us. You can turn them over to us, and be at peace yourself.*

If on a larger, less personal scale, the evildoers whom you must forgive are the social and political power-brokers who terribly offend all of G-d's people and creation, you must speak against them, oppose their actions, vote against them, and do whatever you can to render their evil actions null and void.

But do not cause them personal harm, if you can help it. Do not wish them ill. Pray for their conversion to the common good, however unlikely you may assume this to be.

To forgive these enemies of so much that is good is to recognize them as your human siblings and to pray for a future time and place in which they, or their children, or their grandchildren, will be converted. Pray for a historical moment in which they will turn around and join the struggles for a world in which nations, cultures, and religions are built largely on truth rather than lies and are sustained by energies of empathy, kindness, compassion, and courage. It happens all the time,

---

1. Matt 6:12; Luke 11:4.
2. Luke 23:34.

in every generation. It is happening now. Look around at your own communities, in your own families, at your own lives.

Whether the enemies of whatever is just and good give a twit about you or want your prayers should be of no concern to you, just as it is not to us. Whether such people may regard you as their enemy is beyond your control. You need not spend a moment worrying about how, or if, they may perceive you. Believe us. Through prayer, meditation, the presence of spiritual and political comrades, and the love of friends and family, you can let go of any concern about how your enemies regard you, or whether they pay you any mind at all. Walk away from them, shaking the dust off your feet as you go.[3]

Just hold a space for them in kairos, *which is what prayer is, and get on with your lives.*

---

3. Matt 10:14.

Prayer of Christepona

HERE'S WHAT WE, CHRISTEPONA, *mean when we pray, and yes—does it surprise you that we pray?*

We who have passed on, we whose spirits live with you, as close as your next breath, we who speak together in these pages as Christepona, we pray, and here's what we mean:

Our prayer is a perpetual, often unspoken, outpouring of ourselves, our spirits, our energies, our memory, into our Source, who is G-d beyond G-d, Ground of our Being.[1]

Our prayer is the offering of who we were and are and will forever be to the eternally creative Source of your liberation and healing, and of ours, and of our ongoing presence with, in, and among you.

Indeed, we who are Christepona pray for an increasingly abundant infusion of our power to participate in your healing and liberation, you our human siblings who still live and struggle for justice-love on earth.

And so we must confess with you because—like Jesus and with Jesus and like you—we too are fully human in our histories and in our ongoing spiritual presence with you.

Regardless of our moral moorings once upon a time, regardless of how fervently we tried to work and pray for more mutual, justice-loving societies, we in our families, communities, nations, and world—often we as individuals—conspired, usually unaware, over time and place to perpetuate evils like white supremacy; male gender domination and fear-based gender-violence; death-dealing political economies in which the rich feed off the backs of the poor;

---

1. In his *Systematic Theology* (1967), Paul Tillich developed an entire theological system on this premise.

heinous acts and assumptions of religious imperialism; the slaughter of enemies in war; the ongoing global and tribal epidemics of violence against women, men, children, animals of all kinds, and the earth itself; and simply, dear G-d, in our apathy, our turning away too often from the world's suffering because we were tired, or didn't know, or didn't care, enough.

Once walking, working, loving, and hating in your world, we too were sinners as well as justice-seeking, G-d-loving people on the earth. Oh indeed, we did our best. But we too participated in evil, systemically and personally. We repent the evils in which we participated. And we will repent them eternally, forever, in kairos.

Involved with us here and now in eternity, you who are still alive on earth must denounce these evils in their many, varied, and often seductive forms. You surely know the steep toll evil is taking on those who actively perpetuate it among you today. You must realize that it is taking a massive toll on you all, on the whole of humanity, on all creation, and on the Creator in whose voice we come to you speaking.

And so we who are Christepona pray with you: Forgive us our sins as we forgive those who sin against us because, dear friends, our involvements in evil live on eternally beyond us individually. Although we personally have been transformed through death into a community—a beloved community—we continue to share in the sinfulness of all humankind because we live on through you and carry the burden with you.

We Christepona confess our complicity in evil because we live on among the people and creatures on earth. Like Jesus, with Jesus, as Jesus, we share in your sufferings and sinfulness by being totally and fully immersed in your life together. Those who are fully human must share in the brokenness as well as in the healing power of G-d.

Finally, we Christepona seek G-d's forgiveness—and yours—for letting human blowhards distract us from the joyful work of recreating the universe in transcendent images of empathy, kindness, compassion, courage, and justice-love.

PRAYER OF CHRISTEPONA

This is our prayer. We offer it to G-d, our source—and to you, our sisters, brothers, siblings on earth. May you draw comfort and courage from us.

The remainder of this book, like most of what preceded this last third of the manuscript, was written prior to Feather's death.

Joy and Sorrow

THIS MORNING IN THE pasture Christepona and I are watching the horses and listening to them graze. Still and silent, we see Feather rolling vigorously over and over again, all the way over a couple of times, scratching her back and stretching her legs. We are caught up in her joy.

Joy is a more remarkable and long-lasting experience than happiness or pleasure. Joy is an emotion with staying power. That's because joy is a full-bodied response to whatever is most delightfully good and true, mutual and just, vibrant and open to generating even greater goodness and joy. Lots of experiences bring pleasure and make us happy, but neither such pleasures as good meals, or good books, or good sex, or such happy occasions as birthday celebrations and vacations necessarily bring us the joy of experiencing ourselves in right, mutual, relation with one another—although any of these moments *can* bring abundant joy and often does. We experience joy in some of our happiest, most pleasurable moments. Joy and happiness are kindred spirits.

The thing about joy is that, like mutuality and justice-love, joy generates more of itself. It's contagious and it spreads. Joy is a wonderful emotion among not only humans but other species as well. In joy, we are most alive as human beings and earth creatures.

As in joy, we are also most alive in our sorrow. More penetrating into our very beings than sadness, and usually more transformative of our lives than depression, our sorrow is twin to our joy. These two emotions go hand in hand. Wherever there is joy, sorrow is often not far away through loss, disappointment, or death. And wherever there is sorrow, our hearts gradually can begin again to experience joy through our gratitude for the past, glimmers of hope for the future, and openness to what may be coming toward us.

The important realization for us here is that joy and sorrow deepen and grow together. We cannot fully embrace one without the other. Our joys are seasoned in our vulnerabilities to the sorrows that will come at some point. And when we are sorrowful, we are most vulnerable to being surprised by joy—often when we least expect it.[1]

Watching Feather roll in the late winter pasture is pure joy for Christepona and me. It is a moment in *kairos* and *chronos* foreshadowing the sorrow we will share someday when we lose her if the cancer has its way.

---

1. Lewis, *Surprised by Joy*.

Old Dog Bailey

IN JOY AND SORROW, I consider my old standard poodle Bailey who chose me in 2012, leaping into my car as I was meeting a younger lab down the mountain at the rescue organization. Born in 2006, Bailey survived lymphoma several years ago. These days, he can no longer go up and down stairs, and he is also partly deaf and blind. But Bailey is a source of ongoing joy as well as a challenge to Sue and me, to his younger poodle sister Joy, and much of the time to himself.

    Like Feather, Bailey lives in the present, fearless of the future or of death, determined to keep on keeping on, to try again when he stumbles, not succumbing to whatever fear he may have of being hurt because he trusts us to be there and to take care of him. Sue has built him a carpet covered ramp to get into the house, and our task now is to help him use it without hurling himself off one side as he enters the kitchen door from the garage.

    Every morning Bailey goes with Joy and me to the barn to feed Feather and the other horses and to go for our first walk of the day. Increasingly, day by day, I'm aware of his failing senses, especially his inability to hear my voice when I call or to see me when he finally locates the source of the voice. We bought Joy and Bailey orange vests so we can keep an eye on them as they run through the pastures and woods here in the mountains, and I'm trying to teach Joy to "go find Bailey" when he disappears from view.

    This is probably the tenth or eleventh time in my life I've been mother to an old dog, without a doubt for me one of the loveliest and most poignant—and most challenging experiences. Our love for Bailey holds such extraordinary mutuality for us all, a caring that requires Sue and me to offer all the assurance, confidence, and joy we can, as well as a lot of patience and tenderness toward an old guy who is often incontinent and usually unable to respond to our voices. It requires us to lift him up when he stumbles and to help him into and out of the car. For his part, it requires Bailey to give himself as fully over to our care as he can, trusting us to take care of him. I believe Bailey knows he's as important to us as we are to him.

What do our senior animal companions stir in us that is so heart-rending? What do they stir in us that is instructive, even inspirational? They evoke our tears when they stumble or walk in circles because they don't know exactly where they are, but they also strengthen our hearts if we let them teach us about courage, trust, and gratitude.

From Bailey, I learn *courage* to live as well as I can in the moment, to persist when the going gets rough, to push through my fears of failure, get up when I fall, and try again.

From Bailey, I learn *trust* for those who love me and who encourage me to live as fully as I can, and who ask me to help them do the same.

From Bailey, I learn *gratitude* for present opportunities to shape and share the most precious relationships in my life as they deepen and strengthen.

Courage, trust, gratitude—some precious gifts from our old dog. Bailey.

We hold you and Bailey close in every moment, Carter. Never has an animal been more devoted to a human and never have you loved another creature more than your Bailey.

Hunger, Thirst, and Addiction

LET'S TURN NOW TO *matters of hunger and thirst, which we know you have wrestled with over time and which we can be sure others of your readers have too.*

From the moment you arrive on the planet, you are hungry for more than food and thirsty for more than the most nutritious milk from your mother's breast. But it takes some growing up time for you to begin to realize that neither food nor water nor your mother's milk will satisfy your deepest yearnings to be satisfied by nutrients that cannot be consumed.

This is the context in which many humans become addicts, including many of us in Christepona, and in which most of you have friends or relatives who are addicted to various substances or behaviors. Though it often drags people down into sickness, and too often into death, addiction is spawned by hunger and thirst for soul-nutrients that neither food nor drink can provide.

Deprived of soul-nutrients like justice-love, mutuality, respect, and kindness; soul-nutrients like encouragement for your hearts to dream and time for your minds to work; or, in cases of physical or mental injury and pain, deprived of drugs that might help you—but which are financially fixed beyond the reach of most people—your souls and bodies often become weary and sick unto depression, desperation, or death.

This tragedy of downward spiraling among people who need help has formed the basis of the opioid crisis wreaking havoc in communities throughout the United States. Hungry and thirsty sometimes for food and water, but always for soul-nutrients, and also for safe medications beyond the financial reach of most people, many are lured to cheap addictive substances that eventually will destroy them, their families, and loved ones unless they receive help.

The opioid crisis in your midst today reflects the moral bankruptcy of advanced global capitalism. It is morally obscene and totally inexcusable that drugs are priced beyond ready availability and accessibility to most people who need them. This major crisis in your midst has been sparked by the confluence of inequity and poverty in your society with the profit-driven obsession of pharmaceutical capitalists, buoyed by political pawns, to peddle their drugs, then turn and look away, shedding responsibility and spurning liability.

But be clear that addiction is not only about opioids, terrible as this contemporary global, political, and moral crisis is. Addiction is in the warp and woof of your common humanity, you who are hungry and thirsty for so much more than food and drink. Anyone who imagines that addiction problems are somewhere "out there" and belong to "others" is either in denial or lying. Addiction is always either hidden in your own closets or just one door away from where you live. Your turn, Carter.

Yes. It was early October 1985, and I was lying on the floor of my friend Marvin's apartment in Bangor, Maine, barely aware that folks were stepping over my dead-drunk body on their way out.

A week later, back in New York, sitting in a parking garage, I told my friend Robin that I had decided to stop drinking that very night since my partner Bev would be away for the weekend and I'd be alone. "Carter, listen to yourself," Robin intervened. "You've taught us about the healing power of mutual relation and here you are telling me that you're waiting to be alone so that you can begin to heal? That's not how it works. You *know* you need help. You need to go to AA."

I sat stunned and speechless. I recall just staring at the car floor. Embarrassed.

But I went upstairs to Bev's apartment and called the one person in the world I knew for sure belonged to Alcoholics Anonymous. "Connie, do you know of an AA meeting I could attend sometime soon in Manhattan?"

I still hear Connie's deep chortle over the phone, "Girlfriend, there are only eight hundred AA meetings in New York City every week! I'll pick you up at 8:30 tomorrow morning and take you to one of my favorites."

And so it was that, on the morning of October 11, 1985, I sat with my friend Connie on the back row of a smoke-filled room on the Upper West Side, drinking coffee and munching on a donut. In preparation for this meeting, I had taken my last drink of alcohol the night before. I have not had one since. I owe my sobriety, one day at a time since 1985, to the powerful relational foundation of Alcoholics Anonymous.

Alcoholics Anonymous was founded in 1935 by two addicts who turned to each other for help. Bill W. and Dr. Bob's struggles to recover from alcoholism led them to discover that only together, generating mutuality with each other and other addicts, could any of them stop drinking alcohol.[1] AA originated in these men sharing the relationality at the heart of recovery from addiction to alcohol. Each of them told his story to the other, and each of them listened to the other's story, thus providing the first links in a relational chain of recovery. As other rehab programs have taken shape, many have incorporated Bill and Bob's twelve-step relational foundation on the assumption that we need each other and that no one can recover alone. Recovery is not about our willpower as individuals. Recovery is an ongoing process sustained by relational mutuality, sharing, and accountability in community.

Over the years, some women have critiqued the indisputably patriarchal underpinnings of Alcoholics Anonymous and the various twelve-step spin-off recovery programs. And indeed, AA had its philosophical roots in the Oxford Group, a conservative Christian group. Its founders were two men who understood their addictions to reflect their big egos and overblown senses of pride, personal qualities that Christian feminists often understand as the "sins of the fathers," not of most women in patriarchy.

While individual women can certainly have overblown egos, and while we can be as arrogant, violent, and as involved in evil

---

1. Bergman and Surrey, *Bill W. and Dr. Bob.*

as men, our self-centeredness and pride are usually less defining of who we are, or of our addictions, than men's collective entrapment by ego and entitlement in a patriarchal social order. To lay our problems with addiction at the feet of oversize personal egos and self-indulgence, many feminist critics of AA contend, is misleading to women seeking help in our struggles with addiction. This is a valid and important critique of Alcoholics Anonymous, as it is of all patriarchal religion—notably in the West, Christianity, Judaism, and Islam.

Yet countless women, including feminists like me, have found life-saving resources in Alcoholics Anonymous and other twelve-step programs. We have taken what works for us and left the rest behind—the sexist language and the patriarchal logic that our basic problem is pride in ourselves or that we want too desperately to live as fully human beings rather than in subordination to men.

All of us in capitalist patriarchy, especially in white Western societies, are fed false senses of ourselves as being basically individuals, alone in our problems rather than connected at the root of who we are. Unlike many men, especially white men, many women do not need to be freed from our egos or senses of entitlement. Instead, we need to be liberated from our senses of isolation, especially if we are white. Many black men and women, and other people of color, may have similar gender-dynamics to those among white people—but in America black women and men often have stronger senses of community than their white counterparts.

Regardless of our racial/ethnic identities, women need trustworthy relationships with others who are also struggling to recover from addiction. We need not to feel alone in our suffering. Rather we need to experience ourselves as siblings in a vast relational matrix that affects us each and all, regardless of how isolated our personal lives may be by design, accident, or fiat.

Regardless of the shape of our lives, we are all bound up together in this world. Our lives are interactive and intertwined, regardless of whether we realize it or whatever we may think about it. The wisest among our ancestors understood our interconnectivity across cultures and religions. And the wisest among us today will not fail to grasp this as the most important lesson emerging in the coronavirus pandemic: We are all in this life, this world, and this crisis together. One of the early Christian terms for our interconnectedness was "coinherence," which translates loosely into our living "inside" one another.

We are hungry and thirsty for the soul-nutrients that generate, in Reinhold Niebuhr's famous words, "the serenity to accept the things we cannot change, the courage to change the things we can, and the wisdom to know the difference."[2]

---

2. No wonder that Niebuhr's prayer has become a widespread resource of recovery through Alcoholics Anonymous.

Suffering and Apathy

WE LOVE YOUR PERSONAL *testimony to the healing power of mutual relation. One of the tensions we hear in your recovery story, which we have heard many times, and in which a number of us participated with you, as you know, is the ongoing tension between joy and sorrow, which we have already discussed. Another is the tension between human beings' willingness to suffer and their capacities for well-being, healing, and liberation, corporately and individually.*

Health and happiness are not illusions, but they also are not permanent. Your health and happiness are transitory, because all humans and other creatures suffer both personally and in solidarity with others. People suffer personally when their bodies fail them as they succumb to sickness or injury, hunger or addiction, loss and grief, loneliness and despair or simply the processes of aging.

People also suffer in solidarity with others who are suffering. You suffer personally whenever you yourselves are targets of violence, oppression, injustice, hatred, contempt, or bullying—and you suffer in solidarity with others who are targets of such violence or cruelty.

Suffering is an inescapable dimension of who you are in your human and creaturely experiences of life on this planet. Suffering, whether personal or in solidarity with others, can spark a realization at some level of your creaturely consciousness that you are not alone, that your suffering links you with many of your human and creature siblings. You suffer together with others who suffer. Sensing solidarity, you are able to take some solace in your loneliness or fear.

Short of suicide or madness—and these two are not synonymous and often do not belong together—you have few escapes from personal experiences of suffering sickness, injury, loss, and grief. But you can, or imagine you can, postpone suffering if you turn away from experiencing the suffering of others. This is the way of apathy. You avoid solidarity with those who suffer by taking the path of apathy and walking away from their suffering. Choosing the path of apathy, you choose the way of nonsuffering (from Greek a-pathea).[1]

Let us be clear that all of us in Christepona, and all of you, have been apathetic sometimes, probably more than we, or you, care to admit. It would seem to be the only way most humans can stay sane in your humanity, or so it seems to most of you. We are not putting ourselves above you in our moral critique of apathy, and we have been there too. We empathize with you in your apathy, but we also invite you to consider its cost to humankind and creature-kind. We are asking you, with our encouragement, to choose another path, and we will go with you, by whatever names and images are most helpful to you, whoever you are.

Apathy takes root in your fear of suffering, your indifference to the well-being of others, or perhaps simply in your mental, physical, or spiritual fatigue. Apathetic, you turn away from one another. You close your eyes to the suffering of your fellow humans and creatures. You shun your siblings and thereby diminish your own capacities to experience the power of One who brings justice-love, compassion, and peace of mind and heart to all who stand in solidarity with the sufferings of the world.

Your apathy shrinks you spiritually. It makes you less fully human, less a source of divine love, less who you are created to be: siblings who care and who connect with others who need you to care.

The alternative to apathy is to place yourselves in solidarity with those who suffer injustice or oppression, sickness or injury, loss or grief, loneliness or despair. The alternative to apathy is to seek and find ways of standing with those who suffer—through pastoral care and prophetic activism. If either pastoral or prophetic work is honest or sustainable, these two realms of ministry will go hand in hand: pastorally, to help care for those who are suffering and, prophetically, to help change the conditions that generate or perpetuate the suffering.

1. Soelle, *Suffering*.

You cannot be effective pastors without sustained commitments to social justice because social oppression is always implicated in weakening the human spirit and body. In all pastoral situations, structures of social injustice are somewhere at work, shaping the sickness, compounding the injury, deepening the despair. And you cannot be prophetic voices with any credibility or staying power unless you care about individuals who are hurting, regardless of how you might view their political, religious, racial, cultural, economic, or gendered lives.

The parable of the Good Samaritan, which transcends its Christian origins,[2] is a story about a human choice against apathy. It is a story about a choice to be in solidarity with a suffering sibling. The Samaritan had no way of knowing whether he himself would be beaten, robbed, or otherwise hurt if he stopped to help the victim of violence who lay helplessly on the side of the road. Nevertheless, he persisted in choosing solidarity with the suffering man. The Samaritan, unlike other passersbys who opted for apathy, stopped to care for the man.

In a dangerous situation, involving a foreigner of a despised caste, the Samaritan chose love of G-d and neighbor. Why don't Christians, who cite this parable more than any other, do the same?

Time to talk about immigrants and refugees. "Others."

---

2. Luke 10:30–37.

Immigrants, Refugees, Borders, and "the Other"

NO CONTEMPORARY ISSUE SHARPENS more definitively the horrors of human suffering and human apathy than the crisis of immigrants and refugees in the United States and throughout much of the world today.

The horror of the images almost stops the beating heart. We watch children being snatched from their parents, perhaps never to be reunited. We see a toddler and her father lying side by side, drowned in the Rio Grande. We see other youngsters dying as they try to make it across the southern border of the United States, and still others dying in captivity in the youth "camps" near the border. Beyond the Western hemisphere, we see hundreds of refugees drowning in the Mediterranean and in south Asian waters as they flee horrors ranging from religious or political persecution to deadly gang violence to starvation induced by drought. All the while, presidents and prime ministers of nations like the United States, Hungary, and Australia generate fear and lies to drum up support for closing borders and denying entry to "others" who, they insist, are degenerates of some kind—rapists, criminals, murderers, scum, or simply people who will be a drag on their economy.

But think about your own lives and histories. How do you imagine your ancestors got to your so-called native lands? Even American Indians arrived in the Americas from somewhere else once upon a time and, in the modern world, only American Indians are natives to the land masses you Americans have named "your" country, the United States of America. Those of you who are *not American Indians, however and whenever your ancestors and families arrived—as immigrants, refugees, or slaves—are in truth "the other," those who arrived from outside the boundaries of the land you call home.*

Most of you arrived from Europe seeking refuge from persecution or economic opportunity to make your way in a new world. Some of you were brought here as slaves, ripped from your roots in West Africa, and taken in chains to the Americas. Others of you have migrated north or across the oceans, seeking economic opportunity or safety from danger. But none of you, except American Indians, are native to the soil that white European men claimed as the United States of America.

So how dare you—especially those of you with European roots who came seeking safety or opportunity—brand any other human being as "other" than American and as unwelcome to this land? You do not own the land. It does not belong to you. The United States of America is not your private property.

The borders of the land that you took from those who were here before you, those of you who came from Europe, have no good purpose other than to give you a sense of where you might live on planet earth. The borders were created to give you a sense of home. And for G-d's sake—we are serious—your home should be a welcoming space to weary travelers much like your own ancestors were many years ago, those of you whose families came from Europe or the south.

Honestly, people. The borders of the United States of America have been publicly drawn and redrawn over a very brief two-hundred years so as to facilitate the establishment of a home for people who have mostly come from foreign lands; a home not for some of you, but for all of you—those already here, those yet to come, those coming right now.

Your borders were created historically not primarily as a means to keep other people out but rather to facilitate the building of community, to help you form cultural identities which will be always in flux, and to help bring you together as neighbors and siblings who share a home: the United States of America.

IMMIGRANTS, REFUGEES, BORDERS, AND "THE OTHER"

Why do you set yourselves over and against those who are simply following your example? You speak of "the founders." Well, never did the so-called founders of your nation imagine that their children would slam the door in the faces of other refugees and immigrants.

Never did your forebears propose that your national borders should function as walls either to keep you in—captives in the new land—or to keep out others who wish to come for economic or educational opportunity or for safety from harm. Hardly would it have occurred to your Anglo founders that the United States of America, which they were defining as a new nation—a land of economic opportunity and freedom from persecution—would shut itself off from others seeking safety, opportunity, and freedom. To the extent that such a possibility did occur to the founders, they addressed it through a Constitution that guarantees the structure of a republic, not a monarchy, shaped by democratic, not autocratic, principles. And to the extent that America is a democracy—regardless of how many "others" might arrive on your soil over your first hundred, two hundred, three hundred years—newcomers should always be able to find a welcoming home among you. You should be inviting them to help you build an increasingly open and just society.

This is how it should be working, but it has never worked this way without major obstacles being set in place by frightened white European-American men to protect what they have assumed to be "their" land, their nation, their property.

Keep in mind that the founders of the United States of America were racist and misogynistic. Their vision of a land of opportunity and liberty was seriously flawed by the assumption that economic opportunity and liberty were rights that belonged more or less exclusively to white European males who were already economically prosperous or who were potentially prosperous via family connections, friendship, and assumptions of superiority that accrued to white men with connections.

From the beginning of American history, therefore, all "others" have been welcome to enter the United States only if brought here—or welcomed—by white European males of economic means. This has meant that without white, economically secure, male guardians or "connections," people have seldom been welcome on American shores as immigrants, whether white or non-white Europeans, Africans, Asians, Latin Americans, or poor people from any part of the world.

Despite its founding as a democratic republic and a home for all seeking opportunity or refuge, the doors to this home—the United States of America—have been shut to most people from the beginning, including of course the native peoples whose home this land had been previously.

Most citizens of the United States are here today because, at some point, some privileged white male was either the head of their family or the master—maybe the rapist—of their enslaved ancestors, or because their ancestors made their harsh journeys across seas and deserts seeking opportunity or safety, or because white men drove them from their land and put them on reservations.

Most of you reading this book, if America is your home today, have been "the other" during particular historical periods. Think of it: You may have been here before the Europeans arrived, you may be natives to this land. . . . You may have been brought over in chains from East Africa. . . . Your origins may be Irish, German, Scandinavian, Italian, Chinese, Vietnamese, Mexican. . . . You may be LGBTQ. . . . You may be Sikh, Muslim, Jewish, Catholic, Hindu, Buddhist, Pagan. . . . You may be disabled, old, sick. . . .

The more fully you remember that you yourselves, or those whom you love, have been "the other," the more clearly you may see that your fears of "otherness" are largely unfounded; that those whom you fear need, more than anything, a welcoming place of safety, an opportunity to participate in building America as a shared home. You will see that immigrants and refugees come today, as always, seeking a chance to build a modest life, and to join with their neighbors in shaping their nation and communities as compassionate, caring places to live and work.

Your history as a nation of immigrants, refugees—a nation of "others"—is both noble and sordid; noble in the dream it has slowly and impartially realized over time, increasingly though unevenly a land of opportunity and freedom for those who come; but sordid in its exclusions of people on the basis of perceived race, culture, religion, sex/gender, class, and presumed ability to make economic contributions to the United States.

Yes, it is a daunting challenge—figuring out how to welcome those arriving at the borders of a nation already draped in fear of having too little food, housing, health care, and other resources for those who already live here.

The key to this mighty moral and political challenge is in learning how to share the wealth—rather than continuing to worry so much about owning, possessing, and increasing it. This of course leads us back to Beverly Harrison's musings on capitalist spirituality, a conundrum in which the Christian churches have a major role to play.

What Churches Should Be Teaching, Preaching, and Doing about Immigration

YOUR CURRENT IMMIGRATION CRISIS, *in the United States and throughout the northern hemispheres, is a daunting consequence of two terrible global realities:*

First, climate change *is driving much of humanity out of deserts and droughts as well as flood plains and rising waters toward whatever safe landings they can find. Second,* global capitalism *is creating more pervasive, systemic poverty and aimless, hopeless young people as the result of advancing profit for the wealthiest few on earth. The combined force of climate change and capitalist exploitation is creating global waves of immigrants, especially refugees, on a scale heretofore unknown.*

It makes matters worse economically, culturally, and certainly morally to shut out people who are seeking refuge. Unwittingly perhaps but no less truly, you condemn them to suffering and often death. People of European ancestry should take lessons from your own histories of desperation, fear, flight, and your own struggles to find safety.

So what if refugees are penetrating your borders and finding safety illegally in the United States or anywhere else? Some laws must fall by the wayside in an emergency. Better to be an unwelcome "other" in the United States or Germany or Sweden than a dead Guatemalan, Salvadoran, Sudanese, Somali, or anyone else seeking safety from starvation or the likelihood of violence and death back in their homeland.

But there's not space for more people, you protest. You make space for anyone you love, or you help them find space. You and your friends. America and its allies. You do not throw them away, ever, period.

Your spiritual and political work as Americans in the midst of the immigration and refugee crisis, made more challenging now by the pandemic, has several concurrent parts:

First, you need to speak and act in solidarity with immigrants and refugees by providing whatever you can in your home towns and states and at the borders of your nation.

As importantly, your nations need to be seriously negotiating with people from the home countries of refugees and immigrants to see not if, but how best, to provide basic life-resources from wealthier nations, like America and much of Europe. This effort is underway among the wisest and most compassionate of your political and religious leaders. You, the people of America and other economically privileged lands, must support these efforts with your voices, votes, and money.

Like the Samaritan, some of you provide sanctuary spaces— churches and particular cities. Others can support those who provide sanctuary with your money and time.

All of you can build networks of solidarity in support of undocumented immigrants and refugees in your own communities to keep them safe, to treat them as the neighbors and siblings they are, and do whatever you can to protect them from the violence being waged against them by your governments and by frightened, ignorant, or simply callous people.

Second, you need to challenge the cruel anti-immigrant and refugee policies being put or held in place by the government of the United States and governing bodies in many other affluent parts of the world.

There is no good excuse, no moral rationale, and no economic justification to build a wall at the southern border of the United States, much less to implement harsh and contemptuous policies at the border and throughout the states.

Deportation is not a new problem and it cannot be laid historically at the feet of any one president or political party. It is a systemic problem with a long and complicated history that can be solved only by compassionate political and religious leaders who realize they must be "wise as serpents and innocent as doves."[1] The only way to be so is to work together, across party lines, toward compassionate and intelligent solutions.

Your political and religious leaders today must surely realize that white supremacists, who wield power in your governments, will continue to do whatever they can to stir lies and fear among white Europeans and Americans and to make life as unwelcoming, hateful, and violent as possible, for non-European and non-wealthy immigrants and refugees, especially those from predominantly black, brown, and Asian countries.

Finally, you need to elect political leaders who are themselves bound neither by their own fear nor the fear of their bases. You need leaders who will function as moral beacons, women and men who will work across party lines and religions to design and implement fair and just immigration policies in the United States and elsewhere. These will be people who understand the shape of the countries and continents from which refugees are fleeing—and how to help stabilize these countries economically, culturally, morally, and spiritually so that poverty, despair, and criminal behavior, including youth gangs, will not keep the upper hand.

As spiritual and political leaders yourselves, you must support comprehensive immigration policies that are rooted and grounded in neighbor-love, mutuality, and the wisdom to draw people together rather than continue to shut them out and shatter your common humanity. Be aware and supportive of programs in every state in the United States and in many churches, Protestant and Catholic, and other religious organizations, formed specifically to practice solidarity with refugees and immigrants.

The failure of the government of the United States, working with other nations, to take care of immigrants and refugees continues to be a moral travesty. It is time for Americans to work together, across

1. Matt 10:16.

political parties, to construct immigration and refugee policies on the basis of common sense and compassion as well as honest historical memory of how most of you got here in the first place.

Be wise as serpents and innocent as doves and, above all, be kind, open-hearted, and welcoming to the stranger.

2021 note: The immigration crisis continues under the Biden-Harris administration, although Biden and Harris have made immigration reform one of their chief policy aims, and President Biden has already taken executive action, for example, to protect the "dreamers." The Biden administration, however, needs ongoing demonstrations of our insistence that immigration and refugee solidarity be a front-burner issue. Only we the people can make it so.

Winter Trees: Metaphorical Musing

WINTER TREES REVEAL WHO *you are when you are least covered. Without leaves or flowers, the northern hemisphere's winter trees form landscapes of barren gray and brown limbs and branches punctuated by hints of evergreen against a bright blue sky. These trees have a stark, sublime beauty like yours when you are most open, most vulnerable.*

Winter trees show who you are when you are most visible to one another, least dressed up and colorful, your bumps and scrapes exposed, your nakedness and vulnerabilities there for all to see.

Winter trees are sometimes regarded as too plain, angular, and nondramatic to be beautiful. Seldom, it seems, do people choose a winter treescape as backdrop for festive events like weddings—not only because it's too cold to be outside but also because the charm of winter trees is lost on those who do not view their plain, unadorned character as inviting or welcoming.

You are most like winter trees when you stand upright and show who you are, when you don no special clothes or jewelry, when you are just yourself, expecting no fanfare in the moment from humans who will come later in the spring to admire the elegance of your new growth, green and colorful and lush.

Standing in the cold, waiting for the sun, you anticipate the blossoms that will come with longer, warmer days. Like trees, you experience winter as the season for slowing down and resting in preparation for what will follow when the time is right and the days are light.

Like winter trees, you are likely to feel a little more subdued and introspective in winter because, like the trees, you are not simply waiting. You are taking stock of whatever you may need to grow healthy and strong and beautiful in a more colorful way as spring approaches.

In the seasonal cycles of growth and change, you will not live forever, but for as long as you can.

One of the lessons we have been learning for a long time, Christepona, is that social change, like seasons, comes in spirals, never in a straight line. Even in *chronos* we spiral, round and round we go, and in *kairos*, oh goodness! Our growth and movement is all over time and space, past present future here there converging spinning sparking eternally. Our goodness and our evil come back round forever and ever.

Like the winter trees in a forest, we prepare ourselves, together.

White Supremacy Hangs On

THE ONGOING PERVASIVENESS OF white supremacy is a case in point. We imagine we are rid of it, but here it comes again, looping back just when we let our guard down. Supreme Court justices, some of them, seem to imagine that racism is a thing of the past. This gross misunderstanding reflects how superficially these men—and the justices who share this misunderstanding all are men[1]—view American history as well as the moral wisdom required for interpreting laws across generations. Chief Justice Roberts may not like it, he may not believe it, but white supremacy is not largely in our past, not at all in our past.

How right you are. Euro-Americans have been dealing with the challenges of being white, and of being anything except white, throughout the history of the United States and Europe and anywhere else on earth where Europeans have landed. Those of you branded "white" by birth—a power granted on the basis of ancestry and skin color—have had bestowed upon you a massive amount of unearned social privilege to control money, build families and other institutions, create traditions and customs, including religious practices, and the power to make laws, break laws, and mete out punishment. To be deemed white is to be put in charge not only of how your society functions but also of how you feel and what you think about yourselves and others, those who are white and those who are not.

You who are white have created G-d in your image—He is white, and He is of course a white male (more about this later). You have used whiteness as a measuring rod to determine standards of

---

1. Written before the installation of Amy Coney Barrett as an associate justice in the seat vacated by the death of Ruth Bader Ginsburg.

goodness and beauty, purity and truth. You have deemed whiteness as a "cleaner" color morally just as lightness is usually considered safer and easier to navigate than darkness.

The two most blatantly evil social movements in United States history have been rooted in, and justified by, white supremacy: the genocidal treatment and vicious segregation of American Indians and the transport and slavery of Africans at the hands of white men. These two morally reprehensible, economically motivated, and politically expedient movements and the racist legacies which they spawned continue to be sources of shame and sorrow among all decent justice-loving people of all races, including white people in the United States.

You had hoped that, through the Civil Rights Movement of the 1950s and 1960s, the worst of white supremacy's legacy had been laid to rest, and surely some significant progress has been made. Legal segregation was undone by which doors previously closed were cracked opened to African Americans and other racial-ethnic minorities. Doors to education and voting; freedoms of speech, association, and movement; doors to economic opportunity, housing, and health care were cracked opened—but only barely, and not fully enough to be kept open when pushed against by white supremacists in positions as high as the presidency, the Congress, and the Supreme Court of the United States.

The last half century has seen progress in racial justice—witness the election of Barack Obama to the presidency—but make no mistake, white supremacy hangs on tenaciously in the United States of America. It's in the air you breathe and we breathe with you.

Consider the contrast between Barack Obama's response in 2015 to the white supremacist's slaughter of parishioners in Charleston's Mother Emmanuel Church and his successor's reaction two years later to the march and murder of Heather Heyer by neo-Nazis in Charlottesville. Consider the contrast between the character of Barack Obama himself and that of the man whose racist "birther" claims against Obama helped pave his path to the White House with the vocal allegiance of right-wing media, the ambivalent support of traditional Republicans and their corporate financial base, and the spiritually contorted, shameful backing of much evangelical and Catholic Christianity.

The late great American writer and Civil Rights icon Toni Morrison was one among many who understand very well that a tired old slogan—make America great again—had been dredged up from earlier times in American history and that it has always meant "make America white again."[2] *If the white supremacist revival were not such a dangerous and deadly serious matter, Americans could be forgiven for dismissing these pitiful standard bearers of "whiteness" as hot-air clown balloons that will sooner or later pop.*

On May 25, 2020, several months after I had completed a draft of this book, a forty-six year old black man, George Floyd, was murdered in Minneapolis by a white policeman who knelt on his neck for nine minutes and twenty-nine seconds as three other cops stood by or assisted. Mr. Floyd, who was suspected of having passed a counterfeit twenty dollar bill to buy a pack of cigarettes, lay handcuffed on the ground at the time of his murder. Repeatedly he said, "I can't breathe," pleading for the policeman to let him stand up. Moments before he died, he called for his mother.

A young woman passerby filmed the entire episode on her cell phone, which is how the world witnessed what had happened, and how a revitalized Black Lives Matter movement took off not only across the United States but around the world.

The question lingering as this book goes to press a year later is whether this time things will actually change. Will we in the United States actually deal with the pervasiveness of systemic racism this time? Such a hope is being raised by the enormous outpouring of rage and the insistence on the parts of Americans of all colors and ages that are pouring into the streets, shouting, "no justice, no peace." It is too soon to know where we as a society may be heading, but many participants and observers sense that this time may be different because this time a significant number of the white majority of US citizens seem to be fed up with the hatred, cruelty, and violence that have been targeted at black people since the arrival of the first slaves four hundred years ago.

2. Morrison, "Making America White Again."

2021 note: Americans of color are being met today by an active white supremacist movement that, for four years, operated out of the White House. This movement had once been relegated to the fringes of society and hidden in shame under white hoods, but under Trump it was embraced by the president of the United States and his closest advisors. These men and women peddled white supremacy through their barely disguised white-first, white-best, white-only policies in immigration, health care, law enforcement, education, housing and urban development, national security, and other realms of national business.

Although Trump was defeated in November 2020, his "base" continues, with his encouragement, to promote the Big Lie that the election was stolen from him. The Big Lie was the motive behind the insurrection at the Capitol on January 6, 2021. White supremacists—some shameless and open, but most hiding behind the mask of making America great again, economically, culturally, and otherwise—now hold seats at the table of policy negotiations in Congress and everywhere Trump's besotted GOP still has a voice.

The flaunting by the GOP of conservative evangelical Christianity as the true faith of all good (white) Americans, and the manipulation of this religiosity as a political tool, sheds light on the power of white Christian nationalism as a danger to America as a democratic republic and to decent people of all faith traditions, including Christianity. The most authentically justice-loving evangelical Christians, and there are many, need to understand that the love of Jesus, the poor brother-friend from Nazareth, who lives here among us still, is at stake in this historical moment.

Time Out: Prayer

SOME DAYS AND SOME moments in days call for time out of business as usual.

My friend and Feather's vet Kris has just left. I hang up the halter, call my regrets to the chair of the upcoming meeting, shut down my phone, and ask a coworker to take over the work at the farm for the rest of the day. Then I head home and go inside because its too cold to sit on the porch or the steps.

This is a moment in time when prayer is all there is.

I sit with the dogs and begin to pray—opening myself, stretching toward some thing or someone, some power. I yearn to hear that voice—your voice—when we are rightly aligned.

Please respond!

Listen to us carefully. Kris is on her way home, after x-raying Feather's legs and drawing some blood for more readings of her condition. We know you are tired, distressed at the probability of losing Feather, yet trying so hard to live in the present with her and for her, fiercely resistant to being pulled toward even imagining a future in which Feather is not here grazing in your sight. We know how much energy is required to resist this pull. Do you?

We know how tired you are already, only six weeks since Feather's diagnosis. Do you realize that your devotion to Feather is wearing you out and doing her no good at all? You surely know that you fell and broke your arm down at Kris's barn because you were so distracted by Feather's absence from you and distraught by her illness.

Let us help. Let us bear this sorrow with you, but not only the sorrow. Let us celebrate the joy you and Feather have brought each other, and still do, and let us help you both experience our healing power. Let us wrap you and Feather in our love and let us comfort and strengthen you both, just as you are comforting each other through the deeply mutual bond the two of you have forged.

Feather gets lots of good rest. She always has. You need to rest too. Let us help you.

This is Christepona speaking. Through us, hear the voice of the One for whom we are speaking. We are the brother from Nazareth in Palestine. We are the voice of Jesus and we are also Bev's voice, and Angela's, and Alison's, and your parents, and indeed we are Red's soft nickering joining with all the rest. Together with more saints, sinners, and species than you can imagine, we are answering your prayer.

Let us cradle you to sleep just as we do your Feather.

Rest gently, sleep well, Carter.

May it be so.

Time In: Meditation

SITTING QUIETLY IN THE *pasture together—Christepona and Carter—we are aware that Feather's and the other horses' soft grazing sounds are calming us.*

Breathe in,
breathe out.
Breathe in,
breathe out.
They breathe in, you breathe in, we breathe in.
They breathe out, you breathe out, we breathe out.
We all breathe in.
We all breathe out.
Nothing except breathing and grazing.
Everything is grazing and breathing.
We are here, all of us,
Spirits of living and dying,
together in this one
precious moment in time
(and eternity)
in this one pasture
(and everywhere else)
we are here and
we are now,
comforting

one another.
Breathing in.
Breathing out.

The Tragedy of Misogyny

Too few Christian men or women have much to say these days about misogyny, which is the root of sexism. Like Christians and other patriarchal religious practitioners from the beginning, even most liberal Christians find other issues more pressing, if not more important. And because Christianity, even in its most gender-inclusive varieties, tends to give sexism a pass rather than risk alienating men and some women, misogyny continues to be a driving force, usually masked or camouflaged, in the Christian church.

Christepona is emphatic and angry about this now and always.

Misogyny, woman-hating, is the foundation of sexism, and it is also a foundation of the Christian church. Misogyny is an ancient and universal motivation for social injustice and systemic oppression of women and violence against women.

But why? Why do so many men hate and violate women? And why do so many women hate yourselves and one another? And why do you women, as well as men who genuinely love you, want anything to do with misogynist religious practices?

Think about how outrageous and ludicrous it is.

It's been argued that men are jealous of women's procreative power, even though Freud reversed this jealousy under his male-fantasy rubric of "penis envy." It's been suggested that men resent having to take care of women, having to provide for them financially, having to protect them from predatory men, having to watch over them, as if they were children, having to keep them from making bad decisions about how to live their own lives.

It's been noticed that some men are both attracted to, and repelled by, women's sexuality—and that they blame women for their own sexual ambivalence and shame. Raping women is how such men often express the tension between their attraction and revulsion.

Perhaps men are angry because they experience themselves as doing all the hard work, the heavy lifting, providing all the financial support in marriage for women and children. Another of the most common justifications of men's rage against women is men's assumption that "their" woman is literally their property, which had better not be messed with by any other man or woman.

World history tells a terrible story of men's domination of, and violence against, women. Not all men and not all women, of course, but dreadfully large numbers of men—and many women as well—believe that men should be in control of women's lives, sexualities, child-bearing, choices, economic security; and, furthermore, that if women resist men's control, they deserve to be punished in some way, including being beaten and often killed, not only in "honor killings" in some fundamentalist patriarchal religious homes but, more often, in spontaneous fits of violent rage by husbands and boyfriends in all parts of the United States and elsewhere in the world.

The misogyny undergirding male domination and violence is implicit, in places explicit, in most of the world's major religions, including the three great western monotheistic and patriarchal traditions—Judaism, Christianity, and Islam—which trace their common ancestry to the patriarch Abraham. Each of these religious traditions espouses male headship over women and women's submission to men in the family and, by extension, throughout their public and private lives in whatever nations and cultures their religions are prominent.

Make no mistake: Christianity has codified male domination, misogyny, and sexist theology by building its core teachings around the almighty power of a Father G-d and the special place of his only son Jesus at his right hand. Although women were the first witnesses to the power of Jesus' resurrected presence and were among the leaders in the early church, women's voices and the contributions of women's work—with the exception of Mary and her vocation as a virgin (nonsexual) mother—until recently, have been all but erased within Christian history, both before and since the Reformation.

TEARS OF CHRISTEPONA

The beauty and power of women and girls, their full humanity and participation in divinity, has been largely denied or ignored by most mainstream Christianity for most of the church's two thousand years. Women have been denounced, destroyed, or simply ignored as subjects of their own lives. The creativity and genius of all the mothers, wives, lovers/sexual beings, partners, sisters, daughters, friends, healers, teachers, cooks, farmers, artists, musicians, composers, writers, spiritual companions, pastors, prophets, nuns, and colleagues have been routinely shelved under the rubric of "auxiliary" and simply bypassed by centuries of Christian scholars, bishops, priests, pastors, teachers, and other churchmen seeking to understand Christian history and theology.

To say that the Christian church has had little to no positive impact on women's struggles for liberation in the secular world during the past one-hundred-fifty years in America and in the West is an understatement. More often than not, the churches have actively opposed the liberation of women from traditional roles and in relation to birth control and abortion. It is no wonder that countless women, more than will ever be known, left the church during the twentieth century and continue, more and more, to leave to this very day. Many women and girls, seeking healing and liberation from the damages of misogyny, realize that they must leave the church behind for the sake of their own well-being and that of their daughters and other women and girls. The wisest people, women and men, have realized that the well-being of men and boys is also at stake in this tragic, gendered drama.

Sexism and the misogyny that holds it in place has been and continues to be a global tragedy, a cross-cultural narrative of abuse and trivialization that makes every woman who resists it either a "bad" woman who must be punished, scorned, or ignored—or a liberated woman and role model for girls who want nothing to do with sexism and misogyny and who must step beyond the boundaries of patriarchal logic and religion to live sane and grateful lives.

In this misogynistic world, the possibility of women's liberation depends, more than anything, on women's control of their own bodies, sexualities, and procreative possibilities. This is why the availability of birth control, including the often sad option of abortion, is key to women's well-being. Women can hope that abortion is rare, but they must insist that it be safe, legal, and available to all women and girls, regardless of race, religion, and class.

That there continues to be fierce opposition to abortion in the United States says more about the tragedy of misogyny at the center of patriarchal religion—especially Christianity in the United States—than about respect for unborn babies, a "respect" that is largely a sham.

How can anti-abortion activists square their passion for the unborn with their indifference to the caging of babies and the deaths of captive children at the southern border of the United States? Not to mention that the well-being of children, once they are born, has been of little concern to the very legislators who have been most adamantly opposed to killing the unborn. As former Massachusetts Congressman Barney Frank famously quipped, "Conservatives believe that, from the standpoint of the federal government, life begins at conception and ends at birth."[1]

Christepona—who in the above piece on misogyny rings in my ears like Beverly Harrison, Sue Hiatt, and Alison Cheek's powerful feminist voices—insists that I finish this section on misogyny, starting here with a childhood memory.

When I was six, I overheard a man talking to my father about the Catholic church's teaching that, if a choice had to be made, a pregnant woman should sacrifice herself rather than her unborn child. In that moment, Daddy and I were sitting on a stone wall outside the hospital in Hendersonville, North Carolina, waiting for news of my baby brother's birth. Daddy later told me he was appalled by what this man was saying. Me too. I was upset: why would my mother be less important than the baby—my mother, an already-born person, mother to me, wife to Daddy, daughter to my Nana? Why, if a choice had to be made, would an unborn

---

1. I've been unable to discover to whom Barney Frank made this quip, probably in 2010 or 2011, but it seems to be more or less universally attributed to him by people on all sides of the political spectrum. Twitter continues to "tweet" about it even as this book goes to press.

baby be of greater value than my mother—to God or anyone? Daddy and I were both horrified on that day in October 1951, and I am no less so today.

I have no doubt that this early memory of Christian misogyny secured a place in my consciousness as a Christian girl who would never forget that the church really doesn't care about women, not enough about women as fully human persons, able to exercise reason, able to exercise independence, able to exercise moral wisdom, able to make wise and good choices, and valuable enough to be protected.

The Roman Catholic church does not recognize women's moral agency, but not only the Roman Catholic church. No Christian churches that perpetuate patriarchal images and teachings about the relationship between men and women in family, church, and world recognize women as fully human reflections of the image of God in her wisdom.

This is why, of course, it has never surprised me that churches, on the whole, have never been strong advocates for women's right to birth control, much less safe, legal abortion, as a basic component of health care for women. Only the most liberated Protestant churches in the West have been willing—and only in the past half-century—to resist the misogyny of male-stream religious and social norms. Nonetheless, if we have anything whatsoever to do with Christianity, Judaism, or Islam, and if we are advocates of women's health and well-being, we must insist on women's complete control of our own bodies and procreative choices.

A feminist leader, probably either Flo Kennedy or Gloria Steinem, suggested some time back that "if men could get pregnant, abortion would be a sacrament."[2] It's a simple truth that shocks sensibilities because it reflects how deeply conditioned we are by patriarchal religious "manners" and more basically by assumptions about the value of women's lives, bodies, and choices.

There's something else that needs to be said.

In early February 2020 I laid this manuscript aside for about a month, to give it room to breathe. I took a break from writing so

2. Brockes, "Gloria Steinam."

that I could return to the manuscript refreshed and ready to better assess its worth to me, and maybe others. During this period, as the Democratic presidential primary contests began to be played out in Iowa, New Hampshire, Nevada, South Carolina, and the large number of "Super Tuesday" states, it became painfully clear to me that my candidate, Elizabeth Warren, was slipping away dramatically in every contest. There was no way no explain this, no reason for it—except that misogyny was messing with the minds of even progressive Democrats.

In one of her last debates, for example, Warren tore into Michael Bloomberg, a billionaire Independent candidate for the presidency, who had entered the race late as a Democrat and, in Elizabeth Warren's opinion, was an unprincipled opportunist. Warren seriously believed Bloomberg would be an awful nominee, and she made it clear. Many otherwise liberal Democrats, women and men who had supported Warren earlier in the season, were appalled by her put-down of Bloomberg. Why? I wondered. Was she not lady-like? Was she rude? Was she coming across as a bitch?

Several weeks later, after Warren withdrew from the race, my own feminist brother, Robbie, a progressive lover of all creatures great and small, admitted to me that it had finally occurred to him that Warren was doing to Bloomberg exactly what she would have done to Trump in the presidential debates had she become the nominee. She would have devastated him, which my brother and many Americans, including my brother, would have cheered. Robbie admitted, "It was misogyny that formed even my experience—and I'm a feminist—of Elizabeth's aggressive, in your face, power-play. I had loved her up 'til then, and I'd have cheered if any man on the stage had done what she did."

This story suggests that even feminist, justice-loving women and men, like Robbie Heyward, can fail to notice the extent to which misogyny shapes our perceptions and attitudes. Sexism and misogyny, like white supremacy, are simply in the air we breathe, and none of us, women or men, are personally unaffected by it. Our bodies and psyches are infused by an elusive, everlasting, fearful contempt for women's power.

TEARS OF CHRISTEPONA

Wise women and men can wish that it were not so, but we cannot deny it. We can do our best to challenge it at every turn as long as there is breath in our bodies, but we cannot pretend it away. The best ways to defeat misogyny are to insist publicly on policies that support women's lives—access to safe, legal, affordable reproductive options, including abortion, being a necessary component of social justice for women—and to celebrate women's power and beauty at every opportunity, beginning with lifting up the value, beauty, and power of every child born among us, no exceptions.

Nonbinary Gender and Sexuality

WOMEN'S LIBERATION AND MATTERS *of gender and sexual justice have the same root, because gender and sexual violence against women and LGBTQ people is rooted in misogyny and male supremacy, the presumed right of men to dominate women and to violate "deviant" men who "act" like women or who aren't "real" men.*

Questions about your genders and sexualities stir all humans deeply at the core of your common humanity and creatureliness. You are all gendered, sexual beings and your genders and sexual identities are not as simple and clearly defined as you, and others, once might have imagined, and still might wish.

You've long been taught by religion, culture, and family that there are two genders—male and female. More recently, until the latter part of the twentieth century, you were taught nothing about sexual "orientation." In accordance with traditional Western monotheistic religions, everyone presumably had one and only one "orientation." You were all, naturally, "heterosexual." "Homosexuality" wasn't considered a real, legitimate, or morally viable orientation according to most traditional Christian teachings about sexuality, but rather was held to be an aberration, a sickness, and, if actually practiced, a sin. The idea of two sexual "orientations"—heterosexual and homosexual—was a modern development over the last half of the twentieth century in America and Europe. Today, the idea of two sexual "orientations" seems like a quaint notion.

As recently as the last quarter of the twentieth century, even in liberation circles within Christian and Jewish communities in the United States and Europe, there were only two genders and two sexual orientations. In the realm of gender, a "transsexual" or "transgender" man was someone who had been born *"in a woman's body"* but had never been at home, never had been himself as long as he had lived as an embodied woman. In the arena of sexuality, a *"bisexual"* person was someone attracted to both genders, but often was suspected by other gay people of being a gay man or lesbian who couldn't make up their mind or who was afraid of coming out.

In the 1950s and 1960s, and certainly following the Stonewall riots in 1969, both gender and sexuality were conceptualized as binary. Folks were one or the other, either male or female, not both; either gay or straight, not both. This continued to be more or less the case in most LGBT communities from the 1970s until the 2000s, when the queer movement took off among gender and sexuality scholars and activists.

In the twenty-first century, among Americans and others, "queer" has become a signal-word for nonbinary experiences, and for signaling both gender and sexual identities that don't fit neatly into binary boxes. Over the last twenty or so years, many younger peoples' perceptions of their genders and sexualities have broadened and deepened until now there seem to be ever more ways of identifying as gendered and sexual beings.

No longer are you only female or male or simply gay or straight. Increasingly queer, many experience yourselves moving along spectrums between male and female and between gay and straight. More and more of you experience yourselves as both male and female rather than as one or the other.

However static or fluid you may experience your genders, many of you also experience your sexual identities as open to varieties of eroticism and sexual activity.

In overlapping realms of gender and sexuality, the basic moral questions for many people is how to say or be who you are honestly, whatever your genders; and how to build honest, just, loving, mutual relationships with others, including your sexual partners, regardless of anyone's gender or sexual identity.

Ethics are systems, or rules, crafted to help you make good, moral choices. Morality is about how you actually can create right, mutually empowering, justice-loving relationships. Toward this end, sexual ethics, or sexual moral theologies, have little to do with whether you are male, female, or both; and whether you are straight, gay, bisexual, pansexual, asexual, or persons with some other forms of erotic and sexual yearning.

Sexual ethics help guide your decisions about with whom, and how, to express yourselves sexually in mutually empowering, justice-loving ways—for example, never with children; not in situations where you or your partners are lying; never intentionally hurting or humiliating your sexual partners.[1]

In some cultures, including some indigenous American tribes, queer is normal, even revered. In much of the Western world, however, wherever patriarchal religions reign, queer people—gender nonconformists and nonbinary siblings—know about hate, because you who are queer receive so much of it.

You are hated because you do not fit neatly into gender boxes. You are too masculine, not masculine enough, too feminine, not feminine enough, too hard, too soft, too fat, too thin, too dark, too light, too tall, too short, too vocal, not vocal enough, too angry, not angry enough, and on it goes, just plain too queer. You are hated because, regardless of how much hate is thrown at you, nevertheless you persist; around the world, you persist. You are hated because you refuse to disappear or calm down or make an unjust truce with those who would control, change, or silence you through intimidation, harm, or death.

You queers—you gender nonconformists of all sexualities and genders—have a common moral charge: to learn how to be good lovers. This means helping each other learn your ways beyond the hatred that is all around you so that you become better lovers of yourselves, other humans, and the world.

Gender and sexual identities ought not to be sources of shame and secrecy. They will be, however, as long as you live in psycho-spiritual bondage to traditional Christian and other patriarchal religious teachings that promote binary, either-or, thinking about all matters of gender and sexuality. Your moral task is to break free from this bondage and find your true selves, so that you can more honestly and joyfully love one another as you do yourselves—and

1 Hunt, et al., *Good Sex*.

so that you can help create a world in which others can live freely as themselves.

I've often said that, in her senior years, my mother, who died at ninety-four in 2009, was one of the queerest people I knew: a white southern Christian heterosexual woman, mother, widow, and outspoken advocate for the LGBTQ movement and for struggles for racial, gender, and economic justice, a queer—in the classic sense, odd—Southern lady, not giving a damn in her later years what people thought of her politics or her moral compass.

Thanks to your healing and liberating energies, Christepona, we all have a chance to be a little more queer—maybe nonbinary, but certainly odd in our outlooks about gender, sexuality, and many other matters. For you are the queerest among the queer, bending and stretching and exploding our categories of gender, sexuality, race, religion, species, age, profession, and other boxes we have constructed for ourselves. You are encouraging and empowering us to come out ever more fully to god, to live justice-loving, honest lives in your joyful Spirit, and to help others do the same.

A final reflection on queerness. In Western societies, and increasingly globally, we are experiencing an urban-rural divide in our political and moral perceptions. In America, we are increasingly blue (more urban) and red (more rural). Along these lines, those who write and read this very blue book will be dismissed by our more conventional siblings as elitist and out of touch with "real"—red—Americans.

In realms of gender and sexuality, however, the wisest among us will not fall for this divide. Because queerness is not about who is blue or red. Queerness cuts deeply into all families and communities across lines of class, race, religion, cities, suburbia, and farmlands.

The real question is whether we will be guided by our fears, which are old and tenacious, or by the invitation, the frightening, liberating call by Christepona, to remember who we are—as my faithful, ever-loving sister, Ann Heyward, so often says. It means to break free of pretenses and lies, to be who we were created to be, to live justice-loving lives in the bold, compassionate, and wonderfully queer Spirit of God.

Savagery

ALBERT SCHWEITZER BECAME A *vegetarian only in his last years; yet he believed that meat eating was a form of savagery shared by carnivorous animals and human beings. Schweitzer understood that animals are no less valuable to the whole of creation than humans and that eating them demands moral accountability.*

If you agree with Albert Schweitzer, you'll realize that eating animal flesh raises moral questions: Is it right to eat meat? Under what circumstances is it right to eat meat? What kinds of meat is it more or less right, or wrong, to eat? How does the way animals are grown, killed, or prepared inform the morality of your eating or not eating meat? How does who you are—your health, religious beliefs, the circumstances of your lives and what your options for food may be—inform the morality of your eating or not eating meat?

While each of these concerns frames the question of whether to eat meat, and each has its own moral root, there is the fundamental question itself of how humans can morally justify eating any flesh when, in fact, the human species does not need meat of any kind to survive, or thrive, physically.

We, Christepona, can imagine readers raising arguments on behalf of meat as it pertains to human health requirements and even to the meat industry itself. By the meat industry, we mean the presence of many millions of animals on this planet being farmed solely in order to be eaten by millions of people, and in order to provide income for millions of people, and in order to secure wealth for a smaller number of people at the top of the economic pyramids of your global, national, and local cultures.

Meat eating is not only one of the most pleasurable of all activities for those who enjoy it, but moreover it is surely one of the most lucrative, profit-driven businesses on earth. Two months into the coronavirus crisis in the United States, loud alarms went off from the White House, warning that the closure of the largest meat packing factories in the nation would bring down the massive agricultural-industrial structure which supports the American economy.

Truth to tell, meat eating, like the savagery it reflects, is a staple of advanced global capitalism and of nearly all economic systems as far back as human history is recorded. Along the way, some religious communities, small cultural movements, and individuals of conscience have raised up vegetarian and vegan options and moral matters about food in general, including questions about nutrition, consumption, and the growth and distribution of food.

We who are Christepona cannot overemphasize the importance of this issue. We realize the difficulties that questions about eating meat raise for most of you who have grown up enjoying meat and believing you need it for nutrition. Moreover, we certainly do not imagine that the creation of a meat-free world is anything other than a utopic dream for those who recognize its importance. But those of you who do share this moral concern, individually and collectively, can do a great deal toward building cultures of respect for all life. This you can do by consuming fewer animal products including meat, and by monitoring the treatment of animals of all species regardless of where and how your lives intersect with theirs. If you take seriously the responsibility to advocate for animal well-being, you will probably stop eating them, but you will surely stop doing business with the large agribusinesses that treat animals not as sentient beings but merely as products to be fattened, slaughtered, marketed, and sold to the highest bidders.

The manufacturing of animals has become a morally reprehensible feature of advanced capitalist societies. Know that we go with you on your utopic mission if you choose to resist this ruthless megabusiness. Our strength is yours for the asking.

Truth and Lies

2021 NOTE: THE FOLLOWING section was written in response to Donald Trump's large landscape of lying, his portrayal of major reputable news sources as "fake news," and his assaults on truth throughout his presidency. I've decided to leave it exactly as it was written early in 2020. Suffice it to say that the plethora of lies generated by Trump left a damaged, dangerous, and deadly political culture in which, following his defeat, his "base" has been waging a violent war against the truth that Trump lost the presidency. This piece is no less urgent today than before.

There is something you must say out loud and say often, and you must insist that public figures join you—journalists, artists, religious and business leaders, educators. The time is up for tolerating all the president's lies. The people of the United States are being lied to again and again, habitually and purposely, by a disturbed man who is a pathological liar.

This is not normal. It is a morally bankrupt presidency. Not only do people with good sense not "respect the office," as some presidential apologists have urged. Most Americans regard the man and the office with anger, sorrow, disgust, and shame.

Thus have Americans entered a land of lies and madness, a land of the "double-speak" described by George Orwell in 1984 (1949), in which the world is turned upside down by maliciously manufactured, purposeful confusion about truth and falsehood. The reversal of truth and lies is deliberately manipulated by the shapers of foreign and domestic policies. As in Orwell's dystopian fiction, truth is presented by Big Brother as fake news, and lies are presented as truth. Everything is flipped upside down, including peoples' confidence in their own abilities to make meaning of what is happening around and within them.

For those who wonder why a significant minority of Americans support the mad liar regardless of what he says or does, think about it, which is what Orwell did in 1984. Big Brother controls their minds. He has stripped these people, his base, of their confidence to make meaning of their lives without him. He has lured them, like children, to turn themselves over to his judgment and protection. What we see here is a larger-scale, more consequential example of the merger of pathology and evil than what underlay the murderous events in Jonestown, Guyana, in 1978, when another demagogue, Jim Jones, convinced hundreds of followers to drink Flavor Aid laced with cyanide.

In this cult-like ethos that has wrapped itself around the minds and bodies of a segment—a distinct, large minority—of United States citizens, most morally alert citizens, neighbors, workers, colleagues, friends, and civic leaders become exhausted simply trying to understand what is happening and what their best responses might be in an evil situation that is getting worse.

How do you combat the lies and the evil without harming those whose sad gullibility, or indifference, to the lies are holding the evil in place?

In order to respond to this contemporary crisis, you need to realize that the United States has a checkered history when it comes to the mingling of truth and lies. You need to see that lying, even in the presidency, didn't originate with one man. If you hope to make a difference in your communities going forward, you must accept—not deny—the fact that the problems didn't begin with the 2016 election and they will not end with Trump's defeat or even with the defeat of his base.

Your commitments to truth-speaking must be long-term and they must be carried on by new generations of Americans. This long-term task will fall to the children who must be taught to speak truth to power. At this moment older Americans can model bold behavior.

Among yourselves, you need strategies for the long haul. You need to realize that the United States of America has been constructed on platforms of lying whenever its leaders have deemed the truth to be an impediment to achieving their goals. American presidents, generals, congresspeople, teachers, preachers, and other leaders have often buried the facts and hidden the truth from the people. They have lied to conceal war crimes, torture, and other violations of human rights at home and abroad, and they have lied to justify wars such as those over the last half century in Vietnam, Chile, Granada, Nicaragua, Afghanistan, and Iraq.

Lies and efforts to cover them up are as American as apple pie.

In all of these instances, the liars have deemed truth to be an annoyance. Truth is a nuisance, a damn bother, an impediment, when the goal is to win at all costs.

All the president's lies are especially dangerous because he operates on behalf of an unholy political alliance of white nationalists; profit-driven billionaires; a political party that is hostage to the billionaires and racists; a significant segment of evangelical Christians; and the most ferocious, demented autocrats on the planet who scorn the American president behind his back but compliment him to his face.

We, Christepona, cannot overstate the urgency of this moment. The lies must be unmasked. The liars must be undone and brought to justice. Those who follow them must be confronted and taught truth—not in a spirit of self-righteousness, not by know-it-alls, but by women and men, siblings one and all, who love justice, seek kindness, and walk humbly in the One Spirit of all justice-love on the planet.

Amen, Christepona, amen. In this dangerous historical moment, people of all races, genders, religions, abilities, ages, and political convictions share a major responsibility to push back collectively against those who are attacking truth and peddling lies as "alternative facts."

In order to push back against the culture of lies, we need to affirm here and now that the truth will be revealed, because we will uncover it and commit ourselves to its spread, as widely as possible. We will be empathic, bold, smart, kind, humble, and strategic in spreading the truth.

The truth will come out and it will prevail, because we will create platforms, projects, protests, and opportunities of many kinds, in person and virtually, for the truth to be spoken, shared, and passed on in the spirit of solidarity and compassion.

The truth will rise, an irrepressible power for good, and it will confound its deniers, and we will be sure that those who have purposely distorted or concealed it are unmasked as the fools and criminals they are—and are brought to justice.

So although the truth may be denied, distorted, hidden, and gone from full view for awhile, it will not disappear—because we will not let it die, not in our time.

Like our forebears in the founding of whatever is best in this nation, we are determined and empowered through our shared struggles for truth. We are as committed to unearthing the truth as moral leaders around the world who have waged struggles to make their nations and communities truly great.

Particular figures spring to mind: Harriet Tubman, Eleanor Roosevelt, Cesar Chavez, and Dolores Huerta in the United States; Mohandas Ghandi in India; Nelson Mandela and Helen Joseph in South Africa; and the first African woman to win a Nobel Prize, the great lover of her land and her trees, Wangari Maathai in Kenya. All of these truth-speakers had to contend with cultures of lies.

We will resist fiercely all efforts to normalize lying as the American way, because, although it has had some shameful runs among us historically, lying is not who we are now, not who we ever have been, and not who we ever will be, not at our best.

Aging and Old Soul

THE LONGER YOU LIVE, *the better chance you have of enjoying old age—the emphasis here on "enjoying"! Not that most folks are glad to get old, nor that any one enjoys aging much of the time, because it is not an easy process physically or mentally for most creatures of any species. As many of us have quipped: "Growing old is not for the faint hearted!"*

But it's also true, Christepona, that aging brings opportunities to take stock of our lives and come to appreciate our places in the world and, at least from time to time, to remember inside ourselves the children we once were, to be astonished at the wonders we meet everywhere, not only in people closest to us but among those from different places, people from different cultures, speaking different languages and sharing, if we let them, worlds of different experiences. And of course, we have opportunities, if we are lucky, to mingle with other species and learn from them too—horses, dogs, cats, birds, guinea pigs, turtles, fish, fireflies, black snakes, and the many other creatures, not always friendly ones, we encounter along the way. The copperhead, which seems ubiquitous in the North Carolina mountains, comes to mind. Friendly or dangerous, all creatures have something to show us, teach us, and maybe, occasionally, learn from us.

Strolling along at the edge of the woods, walking stick in hand, dogs running alongside, we take note, Christepona and I do.

There is joy in noticing the great blue heron soaring overhead and the pair of mallards in the pond. Over there are the four horses, striking in their different colors, such a lovely spectacle. A little further over in the pasture are seven white tail deer, including a couple of young ones, their spots beginning to recede. The horses and deer are natural pasture-mates, herbivores grazing close to each other almost every day and, for us, an image of contentment.

What is it about getting old that opens us up to such whimsical aspirations? To be like the horses and the deer, the heron, the mallards? What does aging contribute to such imaginative yearnings? Is it that we know our days are drawing toward an end and, realizing in our bodies and souls how little time we may have, our hearts and minds lead us playfully where we want to go—and have wanted to go all our lives? Do we see that now is the time, the best time, the only time we may have?

Knowing in your bones that there is nothing more precious, you take time to walk, and you pay attention as you go. You notice sublime beauty everywhere and, in a moment of mystical wonder, you see—really see and deeply know—that your lives and values are connected to the well-being of the other creatures who share this time with us.

But why have we come to this just now? Why did it take Jan and me turning seventy in 2015 to take time to walk a small piece of the Appalachian Trail and to aspire to do the whole thing—better yet, the El Camino? Is it simply that we're retired and have the resources of time and money and privilege to do pretty much as we please? Or is there something else?

Have our life experiences up until now taught us who we are and clarified for us how we want to spend the rest of our lives? Are we approaching the realm of old-soul where, like the turtle, we naturally slow down and take more deliberate steps—if we are paying attention? Otherwise we are likely to trip and fall and break more easily, as some of us have learned. But if we are able to lift our feet and place them with purpose as we go, we walk in harmony with our environment. We see who is with us and we often are filled with a joy we would not even have noticed when we were younger. Or perhaps to the contrary, was it not when we were younger that we did first notice what was happening around us and who was with us, the turtle and the wind?

Ah yes, is aging drawing you into experiences of yourselves that are simultaneously brand new and very old? Is this why getting older seems often to take you back to feeling like the children you once were, moments in which you somehow know in your souls that you are actually five years old again, and that you are on your way back, not simply forward? Kairos!

We've lived long enough to have experienced worlds of loss and grief, sorrows and struggles inside and out that have lined our faces, greyed our hair, and worn out various body parts, making us on our best days feel like grayer, wobbly versions of the youngsters and more recently younger adults we once were.

Most importantly, as you move into the realm of old-soul, because you have had so much time to do the work of living, you are sometimes able to more fully notice, and thank, the sacred Spirit living through all creatures, including yourself.

Indeed. In truth, we are joining you, Christepona—and only as we age do we begin to realize it. We begin to hear you and then see you, not as embodied flesh with us here and now but as a presence infinitely more powerful.

Speaking as Christian, I see you are the resurrected Jesus, and the resurrected everyone who meets me now in you, Christepona. Like Jesus, and with him, you are my window into God.

Yes! We are godding with you. We are walking with you now, embodying old soul with you. We are communicating through you, speaking through you, here and now, in these words. Our words and yours become one, here and now, on this path we walk together. We god.

You are telling me that only an older woman could be writing these words, because only an older woman would dare to listen, hear, and communicate them without fear or embarrassment. Is this what you are telling me? Are you saying that younger people might be able to meet you and that many younger people tune into you, Christepona—though they know you by other names and images? Are you saying that younger ones can certainly value your wisdom—but also that aging, especially for many women of all races, classes, and cultures, often offers a generous mix of time and temerity, opportunity and audacity, that can draw older hearts and minds toward what is most important?

Moreover—and this is fascinating to me—contrary to what we so often have been told, getting old can sharpen our minds and stir our deepest memories. Oh, it usually takes us longer to get there, and it requires patience with ourselves and one another but, once we reach it, the memory or the idea or the observation or the analysis is precious and valuable beyond our abilities to communicate clearly what we have found. But when we land upon it and realize that we have found whatever is most true, we must try, if we can, to speak up and share what we have encountered—like the real presence of Christepona who insisted that I allow her to speak to you through me.

And since giving voice to Christepona in these urgent times matters more than anything to me right now, an older woman becomes the perfect scribe and prophet, because neither Christepona nor I is in the least concerned about popularity or appearances. We don't care if our words are heard as those of a flaky old woman. In our aging and in our passing over, those of us who have died, we have learned the folly of trying too hard to please, of worrying what people may think if we speak the truth, of caring whether we are regarded as crazy by those who refuse to take us seriously, or even of being remembered by those who have shut the doors on us or more often have never crossed out paths. Too bad for them, too bad for us.

Yes, beloved Carter. We are here eternally to empower those who see us with a third eye, or hear us with an inner ear, and who know in their old-soul, whatever their ages, whether children or ancients, that we are speaking truthfully of matters that need to be spoken and need to be heard. We know that, indeed, the time for being nice is up—and that it always has been, and always will be, eternally.

Surely your readers know by now that, all along, we Christepona have been your conscience, Carter; your better angels; who you are at your best. We came to you, Carter, in a voice and by a name that you could hear, and believe, and accept as sacred. You know fully and well that we are your window into G-d, just as we were when we met you in the box turtle when you were five.

We urged you to speak for us now, through these pages, and you did, and we are grateful to you, beyond these words of ours and yours.

We will come to others of you, whoever you are, in whatever ways and by whatever names you can hear us or call us. Or we will simply let you be as we fly on wherever we are welcome through all eternity. Kairos.

IN MEMORIAM

Feather
June 17, 2003—April 21, 2020

***

Bailey
November 7, 2006—April 1, 2021

They whom we love
and lose
are no longer
where they were before.
They are now
wherever we are.

St. John Chrysostom, 2nd century CE

Bibliography

Allende, Isabel. *The House of the Spirits*. New York: Alfred A. Knopf, 1982.
Applebaum, Anne. *Twilight of Democracy: The Seductive Lure of Authoritarianism*. New York: Penguin Random House, 2020.
Baldwin, James. *The Fire Next Time*. New York: Dial, 1963.
Bergman, Steven, and Janet Surrey. *Bill W. and Dr. Bob* (1987). New York: Samuel French, 2007.
Brockes, Emma. "Gloria Steinem: 'If Men Could Get Pregnant, Abortion Would Be a Sacrament.'" *The Guardian*, October 17, 2015. https://www.theguardian.com/books/2015/oct/17/gloria-steinem-activist-interview-memoir-my-life-on-the-road.
Buber, Martin. *I and Thou* (1923). Translated by Ronald Gregor Smith. New York: Charles Scribner's Sons, 1958.
Butler, Anthea. *White Evangelical Racism: The Politics of Morality in America*. Chapel Hill: University of North Carolina Press, 2021.
Carroll, James. *The Truth at the Heart of the Lie: How the Catholic Church Lost Its Soul*. New York: Random House, 2021.
Coates, Ta-Nehisi, *Between the World and Me*. New York: Spiegel and Grau, 2015.
Douglas, Kelly Brown. *Stand Your Ground: Black Bodies and the Justice of God*. Maryknoll, NY: Orbis, 2015.
Driver, Tom F. *Christ in a Changing World: Toward an Ethical Christology*. New York: Crossroad, 1981.
———. *Patterns of Grace: Human Experience as Word of God*. San Francisco: Harper & Row, 1977.
Du Mez, Kristin Kobes. *Jesus and John Wayne: How White Evangelicals Corrupted a Faith and Fractured a Nation*. New York: Liveright, 2020.
Ellis, Marc H. *Unholy Alliance: Religion and Atrocity in Our Time*. Minneapolis: Fortress, 1997.
Ellison, Marvin M. *Making Love Just: Sexual Ethics for Perplexing Times*. Minneapolis: Fortress, 2012.
Ellison, Marvin M., and Kelly Brown Douglas. *Sexuality and the Sacred: Sources for Theological Reflection* (2004). 2nd ed. Louisville, KY: Westminster John Knox, 2010.

Ellison, Marvin M., and Sylvia Thorson-Smith, eds. *Body and Soul: Rethinking Sexuality as Justice-Love*. Cleveland: Pilgrim, 2003.

Gibran, Kahlil. *The Prophet*. New York: Alfred A. Knopf, 1923.

Goodall, Jane. *Harvest for Hope: A Guide to Mindful Eating*. With Gary McAvoy and Gail Hudson. New York: Warner, 2005.

Harrison, Beverly Wildung. *Justice in the Making: Feminist Social Ethics*, edited by Elizabeth M. Bounds, Pamela K. Brubaker, Jane E. Hicks, Marilyn J. Legge, Rebecca Todd Peters, and Traci C. West. Louisville: Westminster John Knox, 2004.

———. *Our Right to Choose: Toward a New Ethic of Abortion*. Boston: Beacon, 1983.

———. "The Power of Anger in the Work of Love: Ethics for Women and Other Strangers." In *Making the Connections: Essays in Feminist Social Ethics*, edited by Carol S. Robb, 3–21. Boston: Beacon, 1985.

Harvey, Jennifer, Karin A. Case, and Robin Hawley Gorsline, eds. *Disrupting White Supremacy from Within: White People on What We Need to Do*. Cleveland: Pilgrim, 2004.

Heyward, Carter. *Flying Changes: Horses as Spiritual Teachers*. Cleveland: Pilgrim, 2005.

———. *A Priest Forever: Formation of a Woman and a Priest*. New York: Harper & Row, 1976.

———. *The Redemption of God: A Theology of Mutual Relation* (1982). 2nd ed. Eugene, OR: Wipf & Stock, 2010.

———. *Saving Jesus from Those Who Are Right: Rethinking What It Means to Be Christian*. Minneapolis, Fortress, 1999.

———. *She Flies On: A White Southern Christian Debutante Wakes Up*. New York: Church Publishing, 2017.

———. *Touching Our Strength: The Erotic as Power and the Love of God*. San Francisco: Harper Collins, 1989.

Hunt, Mary E., et al., eds. *Good Sex: Perspectives from the World's Religions* (2001). Rutgers, NJ: Rutgers University Press, 2018.

Isaacson, Rupert. *The Horse Boy: A Father's Quest to Heal His Son*. New York: Little, Brown and Co., 2009.

Jones, Robert P. *White Too Long: The Legacy of White Supremacy in American Christianity*. New York: Simon & Schuster, 2020.

Kohanov, Linda. *Riding Between the Worlds: Expanding Our Potential Through the Way of the Horse*. Novato, CA: New World Library, 2003.

L'Engle, Madeleine. *A Wrinkle in Time*. New York: Macmillan/Ariel, 1962.

LeGuin, Ursula K. *The Eye of the Heron* (1978). New York: Bantam, 1984.

Lewis, C. S. *Surprised by Joy: The Shape of My Early Life* (1955). San Francisco: HarperOne, 2017.

Lorde, Audre. *Sister Outsider: Essays and Speeches*. New York: Crossing, 1984.

McCormick, Adele von Rust, PhD, Marlena Deborah McCormick, PhD, and Thomas E. McCormick, PhD. *Horses and the Mystical Path: The Celtic Way of Expanding the Human Soul*. Novato, CA: New World Library, 2004.

McFague, Sallie. *Super, Natural Christians: How We Should Love Nature*. Minneapolis: Fortress, 1997.
Merton, Thomas. *The Seven Storey Mountain* (1948). New York: Harvest, 1998.
Mollenkott, Virginia Ramey. *Omnigender: A Trans-religious Approach*. Cleveland: Pilgrim, 2001.
Morgurgo, Michael. *War Horse*. New York: Scholastic, 1982.
Morrison, Toni. "Making America White Again." *The New Yorker*, November 21, 2016. https://www.newyorker.com/magazine/2016/11/21/making-america-white-again.
O'Donohue, John. *Anam Cara: Spiritual Wisdom from the Celtic World*. London: Bantam, 1997.
Oliver, Mary. *New and Selected Poems*, vols. 1 and 2. Boston: Beacon, 2005.
Orwell, George. *1984*. New York: Signet, 1949.
Pollan, Michael. *How to Change Your Mind: What the New Science of Psychedelics Teaches Us About Consciousness, Dying, Addiction, Depression, and Transcendence*. New York: Penguin, 2018.
Rasmussen, Larry L. *Earth-Honoring Faith: Religious Ethics in a New Key*. Oxford: Oxford University Press, 2013.
Rohr, Richard. *The Universal Christ*. London: SPCK, 2019.
Rowling, J. K. *Harry Potter and the Prisoner of Azkaban*. New York: Scholastic, 1999.
Sandin-Fremaint, Pedro A. *The Holy Gospel of Uncertainty*. Brevard, NC: Lulu, 2017.
Schweitzer, Albert. *The Philosophy of Civilization* (1923). Translated by C. T. Campion. New York: MacMillan, 1949; New York: Prometheus, 1987.
Snyder, Timothy. *On Tyranny: Twenty Lessons from the Twentieth Century*. New York: Penguin Random House, 2017.
Soelle, Dorothee. *Against the Wind: Memoir of a Radical Christian* (1995). Translated by Barbara and Martin Rumscheidt. Minneapolis: Augsburg Fortress, 1999.
———. *Revolutionary Patience* (1969). Translated by Rita and Robert Kimber. Maryknoll, NY: Orbis, 1977.
———. *The Silent Cry: Mysticism and Resistance* (1997). Translated by Barbara and Martin Rumscheidt. Minneapolis: Augsburg Fortress, 2001.
———. *Suffering* (1973). Translated by Everett R. Kalin. Philadelphia: Fortress, 1975.
Tillich, Paul. *Ground of Being: Neglected Essays of Paul Tillich*. Edited by Robert M. Price. New York: Mindvendor: 2015.
———. *Systematic Theology, Three Volumes in One*. Chicago: University of Chicago Press, 1967.
Tutu, Desmond. *No Future Without Forgiveness*. New York: Doubleday, 1999.
West, Traci C. *Disruptive Christian Ethics: When Racism and Women's Lives Matter*. Louisville, KY: Westminster John Knox, 2006.
Westover, Tara. *Educated: A Memoir*. New York: Penguin Random House, 2018.

Wilkerson, Isabel. *Caste: The Origins of Our Discontents.* New York: Random House, 2020.

Williams, Charles. *Descent into Hell.* London: Faber and Faber, 1937; Chicago: Albatross, 2019.

Williams, Delores S. *Sisters in the Wilderness: The Challenge of Womanist God-Talk.* Maryknoll, NY: Orbis, 1993.